Accounting Systems and Practice in Europe

For Margaret

whose sacrifices made this book possible

Accounting Systems and Practice in Europe

K. Michael Oldham

(MSc, FCA, ATII)

Principal Lecturer in Accounting
The Hatfield Polytechnic

Gower Press

First published in Great Britain by Gower Press
Limited, Epping, Essex. 1975

ISBN 0 7161 0267 6

Set in 10 on 12 pt Times
Photoset and printed
in Great Britain by
REDWOOD BURN LIMITED
Trowbridge & Esher

Contents

Illustrations

Preface

The development of the European Economic Community has highlighted the international need to develop some commonality of business practices and accounting systems which have evolved in response to different national circumstances and objectives.

This book summarizes the practices, objectives and circumstances of the accounting systems in the major European countries. It also indicates current trends, and points to the major similarities and differences of the systems.

My thanks go to Professor T. W. McRae of the University of Bradford Management Centre for his encouragement to extend the dissertation from which the book has grown.

Part 1

European Review

Introduction: Accounting Systems in Europe

There are four distinct types of accounting system[1], each of which exists within Europe. Firstly, there is the *macroeconomic* system in which accounting is regarded as a tool in the furtherance of national economic objectives which are set and made known by government. Accounting reports and information are, therefore, produced primarily to provide information for national policymaking rather than for shareholders or any other interest group. To ensure the provision of the information required, a rigid framework of law is established. Within this system the prime function of accountants and auditors is compliance with the law rather than the exercise of independent judgement, and there is a heavy emphasis on taxation accounting.

Secondly, there is the *microeconomic* system. This system operates on the overriding belief that what is good for the individual firm is good for the economy as a whole. Accounting reports and information are produced primarily to demonstrate the efficiency of the firm as a going concern, without regard to any particular interest group. Accounting practice is based upon economic theory, and the legislative framework encourages conformity with sound business practice but does not prescribe rules and procedures. Within this system the prime function of accountants and auditors is to provide information which will ensure the survival of the firm, and there is an emphasis on replacement value accounting.

The third system is that of *uniform* accounting. The overriding belief underpinning this system is that uniformity in the presentation of accounting information is essential. Accounting reports and information are produced according to a standard format to facilitate the compilation of statistics and comparisons. At national level, uniformity is ensured by the enactment of legislation which prescribes a standard form of accounts and detailed rules and procedures. Within this system the prime function of accountants and auditors is compliance with the law, and there is no room for the exercise of independent judgement.

Fourthly, there is the *pragmatic* system, which is underpinned by two beliefs:

1   Accounting's function is to serve business.
2   Business is a nontheoretical, intuitive art which responds on an ad hoc basis to the requirements of the moment.

It follows that the accounting system must be free to adapt to the changing requirements placed upon it, and be comparatively free from legislative restraints and prescriptions. Accounting reports and information are produced primarily for the owners of the business, who are considered to be the best judges of what information is required. Within this system the prime function of accountants and auditors is to exercise independent judgement in the provision of information, and legislation only provides guidelines and not detailed rules, procedures or standard forms of account. The emphasis in a pragmatic accounting system is on the full and fair disclosure of financial information on an independent and self-regulatory basis.

All of these systems are found within Europe, and in France a combination of two of them exists. There are also countries where the accounting system is not sufficiently developed to fall into any of the four patterns. Considerable diversity of accounting practice therefore exists, arising in part from each country's stage of economic development and in part from different national cultural influences.

A detailed analysis of each country's accounting system and practices is given in Chapters 4–13 in Part II of this book. Each country is described in terms of:

1   The main types of business unit.
2   Business records.
3   The accounting profession.
4   Statutory requirements.
5   Auditing and accounting standards.
6   Extra-statutory requirements.

Current trends are also examined. The countries analysed are the constituent members of the European Economic Community (ie Belgium, Denmark, France, West Germany, Holland, Italy, Luxembourg and UK & Republic of Ireland), and two of the major Western European countries outside the Community (ie Sweden and Switzerland).

These analyses are summarized in Chapter 1, where a comprehensive comparison of the countries is made. Chapter 2 considers the proposals for the harmonization of accounting practices within the EEC, and discusses some of the problems involved. Chapter 3 looks at some aspects of accounting that affect the interpretation of financial statements and which are currently under review, eg inflation accounting.

References

1   The four systems have been identified and described in detail by G. G. Mueller in *International Accounting*, Macmillan, London, 1967, pp 3–115.

1

European Comparisons

In this chapter, a comparison of European accounting systems and practice is made in two ways. Firstly, similarities and differences are extracted from the detailed analyses in Part II and are discussed in order to indicate where problems of harmonization are likely to arise.

Secondly, a number of tables summarize the more significant aspects of each country's business organization, accountancy profession, accounting practices and current trends. The tables are referred to in the discussion where relevant.

Throughout, references to the UK include the Republic of Ireland[1], and 'Germany' refers to the Federal Republic of Germany (West Germany).

Four terms frequently used throughout the rest of the book are:

1 Standards; those self-regulatory codes of practice and procedure imposed by a national accounting profession.
2 Statutory requirements; requirements laid upon the accounting profession by law.
3 Extra-statutory requirements; requirements laid down by bodies such as the Stock Exchange.
4 Rules; any combination of the first three terms.

In the discussion which follows, attention has been concentrated on those areas within which major differences and similarities occur. Minor details appear in the individual analyses in Part II.

In comparing and contrasting present accounting, auditing and reporting practices in the different European countries a surprising number of similarities come to light. Although it is true that a multitude of differences do exist, many of these are merely 'stage of development' differences. If it is accepted that a country's particular stage of economic, industrial and financial sophistication may be regarded as a position on a continuum from under-developed to developed, it can be assumed that differences will tend to disappear as countries travel along this continuum towards a full realization of economic and industrial potential. Thus the passage of time is probably the most effective agent in bringing about a considerable unification of practices within the various countries. However, there are also a number of practices stemming from particular attitudes and orientations which time alone cannot be expected to change. Furthermore, if the aims of the EEC in forming a unified capital market are to be achieved, it is unlikely that sufficient time is available for all 'stage of development' differences to be resolved, because of the relatively long distances some countries have still to travel along the continuum.

The main differences in current practices and conditions can, therefore, be categorized as those which may be regarded as 'continuum' differences and those which are attitudinal or conceptual.

Business Unit

In all countries of Europe the main business unit is the limited company issuing shares. However, there are considerable differences in the type, size, differentiation and regulation, and types of shares preferred. As a result of recent Danish legislation, all countries excepting Sweden now provide for both the 'public' and 'private' form of limited liability company. The latter form is particularly important in terms of economic activity in Germany, Holland, the UK and, to a lesser extent, France. The UK is unique in that it has a large number of quoted as compared with unquoted limited companies. With the exception of France, most of the other countries contain a few, very large concerns accompanied by a relatively large number of small 'close' companies. Consequently, the tendency, other than in the UK, is to legislate separately for quoted and unquoted companies. In the UK the Companies Acts apply to all forms of limited company. Additionally, size of capital or number of employees is often used outside the UK to determine whether a company is subject to particular legislation. Finally, considerable differences exist regarding the provision of capital. With the exception of the UK preference is for fixed interest rather than risk bearing shares and for passive rather than active shareholder rights. All countries other than UK, Italy and Sweden prefer bearer to registered securities. Such differences have considerable influence on standards, reporting orientations and legislative priorities as outlined below. (*See Figures 1:1 and 1:2 for tabular comparison* at the end of the chapter).

Business Records

All European countries require statutory books and records to be maintained; the UK, Denmark, Germany, Holland, Sweden and Switzerland additionally require books of account or the equivalent for the purpose of maintaining adequate records. France has the requirements of the *Plan Comptable*, while minimum requirements are included in Italian, Belgian and Luxembourg taxation legislation. (*See Figure 1:3 for tabular comparison* at the end of the chapter).

The Accounting Profession

It is with the accounting profession that some of the more important differences, both attitudinal and conceptual, between national conditions are encountered. There are differences in the exclusiveness of the work performed by the members of the accounting professions, and in their organization, status, training and numbers. These differences form an interface with the standards and requirements – both statutory and extra-statutory – influencing them and in turn being influenced by them.

In most countries the audit of larger quoted companies must be undertaken by state-authorized professional people. However, many countries do not limit auditing exclusively to the professionally qualified person. Generally, auditing is performed by members of a nationally organized and authenticated professional accounting body, although two notable exceptions are France (where auditing is regarded and organized as a separate, somewhat less rigorous, profession) and Italy (where there is no national organization). In most countries the emphasis is placed upon a theoretical training, concentrating on legal aspects. Denmark, Germany and Holland require both theoretical and practical competence to be demonstrated, whereas in the UK the accent has been on professional practice and experience. In most of the industrially developed countries the status of the professionally qualified accountant is high, probably as a result of the business community's realization of the advisory services that he can provide. The status of the professional auditor, however, is not always as well regarded. This may well be because of:

1 His lack of exclusiveness in the work he performs.
2 The prescriptive and statutorily limited duties that he undertakes.
3 The tendency to employ him as a means of certifying the minimum disclosure of information allowed under the company or tax legislation of the country concerned.

Lack of status may be observed particularly in Italy and Belgium. A further factor contributing to this lack of status is often the absence of any developed equity market, because no general requirement for the disclosure of information is necessary if there is no active equity market.

A further difference noticeable when comparing the accounting profession in Europe is the lack, in some countries, of professionally qualified persons sufficiently competent to undertake a large volume of audit work. This has tended to have a double effect:

1 The audit field is limited to certification procedures, as determined by statute, rather than the passing of an opinion as to the clarity and fairness of the financial reports.
2 The statutory requirements for an audit to be performed, at least of any rigorous or expert nature, are restricted to the larger, quoted companies.

This lack of qualified auditors compared with the numbers of limited companies, both large and small, is particularly serious in Germany and France. Italy also has a similar imbalance, but it is ameliorated by the relatively underdeveloped state of the capital market, the preference for internal financing and the system of public holding-company financing by government institutions.

The potential development of the professional bodies in any particular country appears to be tied to the amount of autonomy and independence allowed to the members. Where representatives of the professional bodies are allowed to participate in legislative reform (as in the UK, Denmark, Germany, Holland and Sweden, and, in recent years, France and to a lesser extent Belgium), one can see the emergence of standards, initially in the form of recommendations but eventually becoming mandatory, governing the accounting, auditing and reporting functions. The accountancy profession can play an important part in the development of financial and management expertise within an economy, but if this potential is to be realized to anything like the extent currently existing in the UK or Holland, it is essential that the status of the accounting profession is high and the independence of the auditor publicly maintained. (*See Figures 1:4, 1:5 and 1:6 for tabular comparison* at the end of the chapter).

Statutory Requirements

Many of the differences outlined previously in this summary may be classified as 'continuum' differences since they are largely occasioned by the level of capital market activity, and the extent of business unit development, industrial complexity and professional development. However, it is when the nature and purpose of legislation in the UK and the Continent generally are compared that some of the larger conceptual or attitudinal differences can be seen. In the UK company legislation has traditionally 'set the scene' by consolidating current best practice into statutes, but assuming by implication that the legislation will be regarded as a minimum requirement which will eventually be updated by the incorporation of future best practices. This provides a framework, and the various self-regulatory bodies ensure that the spirit of the law is achieved. The legislation in most of the Continental countries is much more codified and detailed, prescribing the procedures and imposing a rigidity to an extent unknown in UK company legislation. In contrasting the statutory requirements of those countries whose accounting systems are set within a legal framework – Belgium, Denmark, France, Germany, Italy, Luxembourg, Sweden, and Switzerland– with those in the UK the differences can be exemplified as follows:

1 Procedure;
    UK   Assess society's attitude, *then* pass a law to bolster that attitude.
    Continent Having fixed an objective, pass a law *in order to change* society's attitude.
2 Assumption;
    UK   Assumes homogeneity; when increasing heterogeneity becomes obvious, *then* effect a law in order to change attitudes.
    Continent Assumes heterogeneity and therefore legislates *for* it, change usually only being effected as a result of some crisis.
3 Interpretation;
    UK   The law is interpreted according to the *letter*, thus Parliament is supreme.
    Continent The law is interpreted in accordance with the *intention*, thus the judiciary is of prime importance.

The notable exception to the Continental pattern of legislative procedure is Holland. There the accounting system has adopted a business economics orientation and has, to date, achieved a respectability outside the legal system. Thus although the legislative process in most respects follows general Continental patterns, the accounting, auditing and reporting standards are related much more closely to those of the business, rather than the legal, environment. In this respect, therefore, the Dutch system of accounting bears considerable resemblance to that of the UK, which adopts the pragmatic approach, the main difference being that the Dutch system has a more rigorous theoretical basis. (*See Figure 1:7 for tabular comparison* at the end of the chapter).

Standards

Auditing

No country within Europe has, as yet, codified auditing standards although the profession in some countries, notably the UK, France, Germany, Holland, Sweden, has published or is in the process of formulating opinions and recommendations on audit procedures. However, these recommendations are not mandatory, although most of the professions in these countries have well defined codes of ethics which lend considerable weight to them. One of the main weaknesses is that a large number of companies can escape a statutory audit conducted by an authorized professional auditor. Differences exist also in the audit procedures employed in different countries, some emphasizing internal control review and analysis backed up by statistical sampling, and others undertaking detailed vouching and transaction checking within prescribed areas. Thus, in Belgium, Germany, Holland and Switzerland, statutory audit requirements only extend to public and certain private companies, and it is the *quantity* of auditing work performed which is insufficient. In Denmark, France, Luxembourg and Sweden, where all companies are required to undergo a statutory audit, it is the *quality* of auditing work performed which may be suspect. In Italy, where audit requirements neither include all companies nor authorize a national standard of professional competence, auditing may be suspect on both counts.

Reporting

Reporting standards also vary considerably between countries as to clarity, completeness and orientation. There is no standard audit report. All European countries with the exception of the UK and Holland prepare what is, according to UK principles, a certificate of compliance with the legislation rather than a judgmental report on the company's position. In Germany and Denmark where a detailed auditor's report to management is additionally required, its usefulness is limited because of the lack of any publication requirement regarding the main information which it contains. It is, therefore, not possible to establish, currently, a minimum content of information contained in audit reports throughout Europe.

The report in the UK and Holland is geared to establishing as fair a presentation of the company's position as possible and relies to a considerable extent on currently accepted standards of fairness and, in the case of Holland, sound commercial practice. The reports in the remaining countries certify that the accounts forming the subject of the audit comply with the governing legislation and the company's own constitution, the accent being weighted towards their 'correctness' rather than their meaning. In either case the significance of the audit report can only be assessed in the light of the audit objectives and the report users' requirements. Thus the UK report is probably more orientated to reporting to shareholders than any other national system of reporting, although some of the largest Dutch companies follow a similar pattern. 'Fairness' in reporting necessitates the disclosure of all material information, thereby enabling any user to impose his own standards of usefulness on the reported information. The prescriptive legislation which is the norm for Continental reporting provides adequate user information only for those users specifically catered for by the legislation. The auditor merely certifies compliance with the law. Thus, in Italy, Belgium, Luxembourg and Sweden, and to a large extent also in France, Germany and Switzerland, much of the governing legislation is for taxation purposes and there is a considerable temptation merely to disclose a 'minimum' position, that is the most conservative position commensurate with the tax laws. In France and Germany, in addition to the tax legislation, company law prescribes in considerable detail the items to be shown in financial statements. In these two countries, as well as in Denmark and Switzerland, the orientation is towards the protection of creditors rather than towards provision of information to the equity shareholders. Creditor-orientated information does not necessarily fulfil the needs of the equity investor. This orientation is manifested in the emphasis placed upon the balance sheet in most European countries rather than on the earnings statement.

Accounting

Accounting standards range from the flexibly pragmatic standards of the UK, through the principles of 'good housekeeping' and 'orderly bookkeeping' of Holland and Germany respectively, to the rigidly prescriptive requirements of the French *Plan Comptable*. However, the validity of the standards in existence is governed entirely by the objectives of accounting and, as outlined in the previous paragraph it is in the diversity of these objectives that much of the trouble arises. What can be said is that once objectives have been established, there is much to be gained by codifying a set of mandatory standards which will fulfil them. The current position is that whilst the economically advanced European countries have a series of recommended accounting standards, only Holland has set them within a theoretical framework, and only the UK has made any standards mandatory. The rules outlined by the French *Plan Comptable* and, to some extent, by the German 'orderly book-keeping' system are more concerned with outlining a procedure than with instituting standards of accounting practice. As such, whilst they may impose an element of discipline on the reporter, they do not necessarily provide any insight to the report user. (*See Figure 1:8 for tabular comparison* at the end of the chapter).

Extra-statutory Requirements

The system of extra-statutory requirements and controls which operates in the UK is unique. However, in some respects this may well be a 'continuum' difference due to the more recent development of many of the Continental professional bodies, the lack of stock market activity and less developed takeover and merger activity. There is currently considerable activity on the part of the Dutch, Danish, German, French and Swedish professional bodies to issue opinions and recommendations covering accounting, auditing and reporting standards. Thus, one can anticipate the emergence of a fairly common body of 'European' self-regulation in the relatively near future. Whether such self-regulatory bodies will be able to coexist with an accounting system set within a rigid legal framework will, to a large extent, depend upon the success of attempts to define the objectives of an accounting system. Certainly, this is not a problem confined to those countries whose accounting system is set within such a legal framework – the UK also lacks any defined accounting objectives.

In the case of extra-statutory controls concerning Stock Exchange reporting requirements, there are at least three reasons for lack of controls on the part of all the other Stock Exchanges compared with those of the UK. Firstly, the others' preference for internal financing by the firm, or for fixed interest securities on the part of the private investor, has inhibited the growth of equity markets and the resultant need for relevant investor-orientated information. Secondly, the Continental practice of raising finance primarily through banks or government-sponsored institutions, has to a large extent bypassed the Stock Exchanges. Thirdly, the Continental private investor has shown a marked preference for savings banks and institutions rather than an involvement in industrial investment where he feels that he is at the mercy of institutional and business manipulators. The first two reasons are likely to be overcome as countries find economic activity increasing beyond the stage where sufficient risk capital is available from internal resources or public institutions. In the case of the third reason, the need for business to become less secretive in order to obtain the necessary finance for expansion, plus the attraction to the private investor of the possibility of capital gains as a counter to inflation, will do much to overcome the private investor's aversion to equity investment.

There are already Government moves in France and Italy to stimulate stock market activity and in Germany to limit the stranglehold of the banks. However, the assumption must be that in most Continental countries these moves will take the form of statutory controls rather than extra-statutory ones and, in such a case, it is doubtful that they will be able to cope adequately with a rapid increase in stock market activity.

Controls are also beginning to emerge over takeovers and mergers on the Continent, since these events are symptomatic of increasing economic activity. However, here again, the controls are likely to be statutory – as, recently, in Germany – and one must question whether they will possess the necessary flexibility which, it is argued, is the main advantage of the UK City Code on Takeovers and Mergers. (*See Figure 1:9 for tabular comparison* at the end of the chapter).

Current Reporting Practice

The influence of national environments and rules is reflected in the different practices relating to the treatment in financial statements of similar items. Thus, there are significant differences in the treatment of assets, and in the recording and constitution of reserves and shareholders equity. The degree of importance attached to an income statement is reflected in the items to be included in it, and in the nature of their treatment. (*See Figures*

1:10, 1:11 and 1:12 for tabular comparison at the end of the chapter).

Current Trends

In most of the industrially developed European countries there already exists a well-organized accounting profession, actively engaged in establishing and improving accounting, auditing and reporting standards. Such moves are backed up in those countries by systems of company legislation which have been recently reformed or are currently undergoing reform. The main differences exist in the orientations and environments of the accounting systems. Thus, we have seen that many of the existing differences can be classified as 'continuum' differences and will tend to disappear as the need for their disappearance makes its presence felt.

There are, however, a number of more serious differences which are conceptually based and tend to stem from the orientation of particular legislation and from differing views as to the specific role to be played in an economy by accounting, auditing and reporting. Some limited attempts have been made to cope with these differences where companies have had to traverse national boundaries. The growing internationalism of the larger companies has involved establishing 'beach-heads' in countries employing a different accounting system. In the past, this internationalism has been accompanied by a growth of international firms of accountants and auditors, and they have tended to carry with them 'best practice'. However, such a situation is limited to the largest of industrial and professional firms and is unlikely to overcome universally the conceptual differences previously referred to. Political decisions resulting in legislation which will, at least, set the scene within which acceptable and useful standards of reporting can be established are the only 'universal' solution. Only political decisions will be able to overcome the barriers of national pride, taxation legislation and vested institutional and private interests. Current moves do suggest some convergence of national priorities. Thus one can observe moves in France and Germany aimed at liberalizing a previously tightly controlled accounting framework, and a complementary move in the UK towards some restriction of a traditionally 'free' and self-regulatory accounting environment. (*See Figure 1:13 for tabular comparison* at the end of the chapter.)

The overall relationship of European accounting systems and practice is related to the four patterns of accounting described in the Introduction, and presented in diagramatic form in Figure 1:14 at the end of the chapter.

Belgium, Denmark, France, Germany, Luxembourg and Sweden may all be described as macroeconomic accounting systems, the French system also being set within a uniform framework. In contrast, the accounting system in Holland is microeconomic with a considerable amount of self-regulation by the profession. The UK's system is currently pragmatic, being completely independent of theoretical underpinning and almost entirely self-regulatory. The Swiss system tends to be microeconomic but with far less self-regulation than obtains in Holland, whilst the Italian system is not sufficiently developed to fall into any one of the four major patterns.

The European Economic Community is currently attempting to effect some degree of harmonization of the accounting systems and practices of its member states, and these attempts are described in the next chapter.

References

1 The Republic of Ireland is being considered in common with the UK because company law, professional organization and extra-statutory requirements are very similar in both countries. The Institute of Chartered Accountants in Ireland is comprised of members from Northern Ireland and the Republic; stock exchanges in the Republic are members of the Federated Stock Exchanges.

	1 Public limited company	2 Private limited company	3 Partnership limited by shares	4 Limited partnership	5 General partnership	6 Professional (civil) partnership	7 Sole trader	Most significant type of unit
United Kingdom & Republic of Ireland	✓	✓		✓ (Rare)	✓		✓	1
Belgium	✓	✓	✓	✓	✓		✓	2
Denmark	✓	✓ (Since 1 January 1974)	✓ (Rare)	✓	✓		✓	1
France	✓	✓	✓	✓	✓	✓	✓	2
Germany	✓	✓	✓	✓	✓	✓	✓	2
Holland	✓	✓ (Since 1971)	✓	✓	✓	✓	✓	1
Italy	✓	✓	✓	✓	✓	✓	✓	1
Luxembourg	✓	✓	✓	✓	✓		✓	1
Sweden	✓	✓	✓	✓	✓	✓	✓	1
Switzerland	✓	✓ (Rare)	✓ (Rare)	✓	✓	✓	✓	1

Figure 1:1 Type of business unit: variety of organizations

Country	Period of existence — Finite	Period of existence — Infinite	Major sources of finance — Internal	Major sources of finance — External Institutional	Major sources of finance — External Private	Main type of shares — Registered	Main type of shares — Bearer	Transfer of shares is unrestricted	Company can purchase its own shares	Annual accounts — Must be published	Annual accounts — Must be filed	Minimum share capital — For incorporation	Minimum share capital — For stock exchange listing	Supplementary notes
United Kingdom & Republic of Ireland	✓	✓	✓	✓	✓	✓	✓	✓		✓	✓	No	Total market value of £250 000	Minimum market value of £100 000 for any particular security to be quoted
Belgium		✓	✓	✓		✓	✓	✓		✓	✓	No	£109 000	
Denmark		✓	✓	✓		✓	✓	✓	Not since 1 January 1974 prior to 1974 up to 10% only	✓	✓	1 January 1974 £7000 (formerly £700)	£138 000	
France	✓	✓	✓	✓		✓	✓	Normally		✓	✓	£45 000	No	Where company restricts rights to transfer shares minimum capital for incorporation is £9000
Germany		✓	✓	✓		✓	✓	✓	✓ (Up to 10% only)	✓	✓	£17 000	No	
Holland		✓	✓	✓	A few international companies only ✓	✓	✓	✓		✓	✓	No	No	
Italy	✓		✓	✓		✓	✓	✓		✓	✓	£670	£670 000	
Luxembourg	✓		✓	✓		✓	Special permission required - rare	✓		✓	✓	No	No	
Sweden		✓	✓	✓		✓	✓	✓		✓	✓	£500	£500 000	
Switzerland		✓	✓	A few large companies only ✓		✓	✓	Normally		Only banks and insurance companies	Only banks and insurance companies	£7000 (paid up £2800)	£70 000 (Domestic) £140 000 (Foreign)	

Figure 1:2   Type of business unit: different characteristics of public limited companies

	Specified in detail	Detail unspecified
United Kingdom & Republic of Ireland	Registers of share and debenture holders, directors, loans to the company	Proper books of account
Belgium	Share register; official journal; balances book; approved records of sales, purchases and personnel	
Denmark	Minute books; registers of shareholders, directors' and managers' sharedealings	Records for book-keeping purposes
France	According to the national plan and the commercial code	
Germany		To conform 'to the principles of orderly book keeping'
Holland		Proper records for ascertainment of assets and liabilities
Italy	Minute books; share register; records of payroll, personnel, fixed assets, payments to third parties	
Luxembourg	Share register; official journal; balances book; Approved records of sales, purchases and personnel	
Sweden	Share register; the journal; the inventory book; cash book	Such additional records as are necessary
Switzerland	Records must be maintained: 1) For social security purposes. 2) On taxes witheld. 3) For taxation purposes	Proper books of account, adequate for the type and size of operations, permitting the determination of the business' assets and liabilities and the results of its operation

Figure 1:3 Business records legally required

Country		Minimum years needed to qualify post-school	Post-school education			Experience	
			Nature	Emphasis	Minimum time in years	Nature	Minimum time in years
United Kingdom & Republic of Ireland *		5	Full-time, plus part-time professional examinations	General practical, job-oriented	4	In a professional accountant's office	3
Belgium	a)	9	Full-time degree, and/or professional examinations	Law	4	5-year articles with a public accountant, minimum age 30 years	5
	b)	7	Full-time degree or professional examinations	Law and economics	4	At least 3 years practical experience, minimum age 25 years	3
Denmark	c)	8	Full-time bachelor and master's degrees plus six seminars for professional examinations	Economic and accounting theory, practical, job oriented	5	At least 3 years in the office of a public accountant; minimum age 25 years	3
	d)	5	Part-time courses	Auditing, accounting and financial statements		At least 5 years relevant work in an audit firm, minimum age 25 years	5
France	e)	10	Diploma in accounting studies and a thesis on accounting	Law	3	3 years in the employment of an accountant, minimum age 25 years	3
	f)	10	Qualifying examination in accounting and law	Law		3 years practical training plus general experience; minimum age 25 years	10
Germany Either:		10	Holders of specified degrees with subsequent professional examinations	Law	4	Business experience, at least 4 years in an accountant's office or 2 with an accountant and 2 with a lawyer	6
Or:		10	Professional examinations	Law		Practical, with an accountant	10
Holland Either:		7	First degree, full-time; part-time accountancy diploma	Business economics	7	None required	-
Or:		8½	Part-time accountancy diploma	Business economics and accounting practice	8½	None compulsory, but it is usual to have some accounting experience	-
Italy	g)	4	Full-time degree, doctoral thesis, followed by state examination	Law	4	No practical requirement, minimum age 25 years	-
	h)	7	Part-time accounting diploma followed by state examination	Law	5	At least 2 years with a public accountant, minimum age 25 years	2
Luxembourg		5½	Full-time degree	None specified	4	If a business graduate, 1½ years articles and approved experience. Other graduates, 3 years articles with a public accountant. Minimum age 24 years in either case	1½
Sweden		8	Full-time degree, or (rarely) successful completion of examinations set by university professors	Economics, law, accounting, and auditing	3	5 years post-examination with an authorized public accountant, to become authorized. One further year in practice for membership of professional body. Minimum age 25 years	5
Switzerland		6	State examination for membership of auditing chamber, but no requirement for appointment as statutory auditor	Accounting and auditing but also requires some knowledge of mathematics and economics	-	A minimum of 6 years accounting and relevant experience, of which at least 2 years must include auditing experience	6

Key to references:
* Refers to Chartered Accountants only
a) Accountant (Expert Comptable)
b) Auditor (Reviseur D' Enterprises)
c) State Authorized Public Accountant
d) Registered Accountant
e) Accountant (Expert Comptable)
f) Auditor (Commissaire)
g) Doctor of Commerce
h) Accountant and Commercial Expert

Figure 1:4   Accountancy profession: method of qualifying

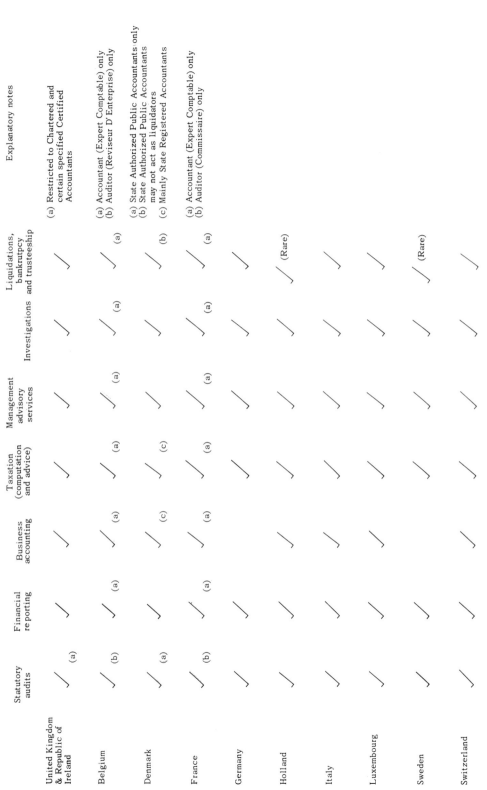

Figure 1:5 Accountancy profession: organization and scope of work

	Legally prescribed rules	Professionally formalized rules	Other formalized rules
United Kingdom & Republic of Ireland	Few; general rather than detailed	Many detailed recommendations; few mandatory requirements	Stock Exchange requirements (detailed and mandatory) takeover and merger code (general and not mandatory)
Belgium	Few and imprecise		
Denmark	Some and detailed	Some auditing and accounting opinions Recommended model financial statements	
France	Many and detailed		Stock Exchange Council and COB recommendations on disclosure, auditor competence, takeovers and mergers
Germany	Many and detailed	Auditing recommendations	
Holland	Few; general rather than detailed	No mandatory requirements; acceptable standards encouraged by Code of Ethics	Joint study group of employers, trade unions and NI v RA establishing standards of financial reporting deemed acceptable to the present social system
Italy	Few and imprecise		
Luxembourg	Few and imprecise		
Sweden	Few and imprecise	No codified standards but some recommendations	Stock Exchange recommendations on disclosure and accounts presentation
Switzerland	Few and imprecise		Stock Exchange recommendations towards fuller disclosure

Figure 1:6   Accountancy profession: source of rules and practice

Figure 1:7 Statutory requirements for public limited companies

	Contents of accounts			Form of accounts		Asset valuation	Consolidated statements	Auditor's report	Directors' report	Orientation of statutes			Explanatory notes concerning consolidated statements
	Balance sheet	Profit and loss account	Notes	Balance sheet	Profit and loss account					Owner	Creditor	Tax	
United Kingdom & Republic of Ireland	✓	✓	✓				✓	✓	✓	✓			Group accounts must be prepared
Belgium	✓	✓						✓	✓			✓	Consolidated accounts are specifically precluded from being substituted for individual company balance sheets
Denmark	✓	✓	✓				✓	✓	✓		✓		No requirement for group accounts
France	✓	✓		✓	✓	✓		✓	✓			✓	No requirement for consolidated statements other than on a new issue (COB). Income and turnover of, and equity in, subsidiaries must be shown together with details of associated companies
Germany	✓	✓		✓	✓	✓	✓	✓	✓		✓		Group accounts must be prepared for the holding company and all subsidiaries domiciled within West Germany, but need not include other subsidiaries
Holland	✓	✓	✓				✓	✓	✓	✓			Accounts of subsidiaries may be shown individually or in an amalgamated form. No requirement for group accounts
Italy	✓					✓		✓	✓			✓	
Luxembourg	✓							✓	✓			✓	Consolidated accounts cannot be presented in place of individual investment company and fund balance sheets
Sweden	✓	✓				✓	✓	✓	✓		✓	✓	A consolidated balance sheet or group statement must be prepared for the board of directors and auditors but not for publication to shareholders
Switzerland	✓					✓		✓			✓		

Auditing　　　　　Accounting　　　　　Reporting

	Auditing				Accounting					Reporting			
	Codified principles	Statutory requirements	Professionally established Mandatory	Professionally established Recommended	Codified principles	Statutory requirements	Professionally established Mandatory	Professionally established Recommended	Auditor certifies legal correctness	Form of auditor's report Long	Form of auditor's report Short	Auditor's opinion required on accounts	Director's report is certified
United Kingdom & Republic of Ireland			✓	✓	(Developing)		✓	✓			✓	✓	
Belgium		✓		✓		✓		✓	✓	✓	✓		✓
Denmark				✓				✓	✓	✓	✓		
France		✓			✓	✓			✓	✓	✓		✓
Germany		✓		✓	✓	✓			✓	✓	✓		✓
Holland		✓		✓	(Developing)		✓			✓	✓	✓	
Italy		✓				✓			✓	✓	✓		
Luxembourg		✓				✓		✓	✓	✓	✓		✓
Sweden				✓					✓	✓			✓
Switzerland									✓	✓			✓

Figure 1:8　Professional standards

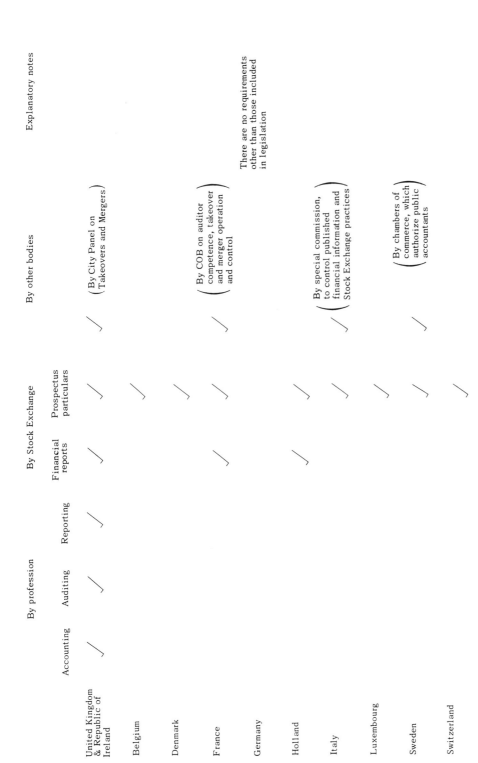

Figure 1:9 Extra-statutory requirements

Fixed assets / Basis of valuation / Depreciation / Investments shown at: / Stocks Shown at:

	Basis of valuation				Depreciation		Goodwill and intangibles write-off period	Investments shown at:			Stocks Shown at:				
	Historic cost	Index adjusted	Current value	Revalued	On asset life	Per tax rules		Cost	Cost less reserves	Market value	Cost	Index adjusted	Current value	Market value if less than cost	Cost less reserve
United Kingdom & Republic of Ireland	✓	✓		✓	✓		Optional	✓		✓	✓	✓		✓	
Belgium	✓			✓		✓ Based On Historic Cost	Optional	✓		✓	✓			✓	✓
Denmark	✓			✓	✓ Based on historic cost since 1 January 1974		1-10 Years	✓		✓	✓			✓	Tax value may be below book value
France	✓			✓		✓	1-5 Years	✓	✓	✓	✓			✓	
Germany	✓			✓		✓	1-5 Years	✓	✓	✓	✓			✓	✓
Holland	✓		✓		✓		Optional	✓	✓	✓	✓		✓	✓	
Italy	✓			✓		✓	Reasonable time or as prescribed by tax rules	✓	✓	✓	✓			✓	✓
Luxembourg	✓						Optional	✓	✓	✓	✓			✓	✓
Sweden	✓			✓		✓	10 Years	✓	✓	✓	✓			✓	✓
Switzerland	✓					✓	Optional	✓	✓	✓	✓			✓	✓

Figure 1:10   Current reporting practice: assets

Figure 1:11   Current reporting practice: liabilities, reserves and capital

	Turnover is shown	Cost of sales is shown	Pre-planned and accelerated depreciation distinguished	Directors' fees treated as: Appropriation of profit	Directors' fees treated as: Charge on profit	Extraordinary items are shown	Operating profit for year is shown	Tax shown is: Cash actually paid	Tax shown is: Accrued liability	Tax shown is: Accrued plus deferred liability	Profit shown is restricted to the recommended distribution
United Kingdom & Republic of Ireland	✓		✓	✓	✓	✓	✓			✓	
Belgium				✓				✓	✓		
Denmark	✓	✓	Accelerated depreciation not allowed		✓	✓					
France	✓			✓	✓	✓			✓	✓	Often
Germany	✓			✓	✓				✓		✓
Holland	Usually		✓	✓		✓	Usually		✓	✓	
Italy				✓		✓	✓	✓	✓		Often
Luxembourg				✓			✓	✓	✓		
Sweden	✓				✓				✓		
Switzerland				✓		✓	✓	✓	✓		Often

Figure 1:12   Current reporting practice: income statement

	Statutory	Professional	Stock Exchange	Other
United Kingdom & Republic of Ireland	Proposed companies commission which will extend legislation over a wider range of business activities; a tendency to move from permissive to prescriptive legislation	Attempts to raise professional standards by education and by establishing codes of practice	Criticism from outside as to its role and functioning	Pressure from outside business for its accountability to society
Belgium	Government intends to adopt a national plan of accounting	Attempts to formulate recommendations of good practice	Attempts by the Commission Bancaire to improve Stock Exchange practice and information	–
Denmark	Company legislation being adopted to improve quality and quantity of published information	Attempts to formulate recommendations of good practice; move towards a standard audit report including an auditor's opinion	–	–
France	Extension of legislation to improve information for investors and to increase stock market activity	Gradual evolution of auditing and accounting recommendations	–	COB improving auditing standards and Stock Exchange practice generally eg re takeovers, mergers, insider dealings
Germany	Regulation of takeovers/mergers; moves to separate tax and financial reporting; attempts to broaden shareholding by involving employees and curbing banks' activities	–	–	Increasing pressure from public shareholders and trade unions is tending to change traditional pattern of ownership and control of German industry
Holland	–	Attempts to establish an inventory of business and reporting standards	–	The profession, employers and trade unions are together seeking to establish acceptable reporting standards
Italy	Company law reform to improve quality of financial statements; establishment of a register of approved auditing firms	–	Move to reform and increase activity	–
Luxembourg	–	–	–	–
Sweden	A new book-keeping law in draft; proposals for a Nordic Companies Act are under consideration	–	New rules for disclosure of information by quoted companies now being considered	Pressure to increase business accountability to society
Switzerland	Committee now considering reform of company law re financial statements, auditor's reports and company capital structure	Attempts to improve auditing standards; working party established to recommend minimum qualifications and independence of auditors	More disclosure of information being requested, intention being that requirements shall ultimately be made mandatory	–

Figure 1:13   Current trends

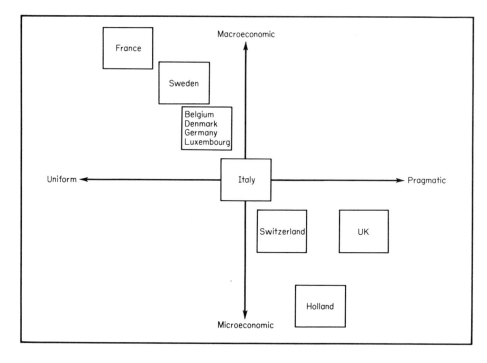

Figure 1:14   The overall relationship of European accounting systems and practices

2

European Harmonization and the Proposed European Company

Introduction

Two of the prime objectives laid down in Article 3 of the Treaty of Rome, which established the European Economic Community (EEC), are:

1 The abolition as between member states of obstacles to freedom of movement for persons, services and capital.
2 The institution of a system ensuring that competition in the common market is not distorted.

If these objectives are to be achieved, information which is adequate as regards both quantity and quality will be needed.

The EEC bureaucracy implements policy by issuing three kinds of instruments:

1 Regulations: these are automatically incorporated into every member state's legislation without any national action being required.
2 Directives: these instruct members as to *what* has to be done, but may require the passing of enabling legislation nationally, to determine *how* the objective is to be achieved.
3 Decisions: these are usually concerned with a specific problem, and are binding on all those to whom they are addressed.

Policy suggestions are made by the Commission (composed of members from all participant states, and presumed to be above national interest), discussed by interested parties
and possibly amended, and finally ratified by the Council of Ministers (the
decision-making body of the EEC, and usually the Foreign Secretaries of member states).
It is at the final decision-making level of the Council that political factors are considered.

The areas of harmonization relevant to accounting systems and practice are: company
law; the law relating to professions; and the establishment of a European company.

Proposals for Harmonization of Company Law, the Law Relating to Professions, and Other Related Matters

Profit and Loss Account and Balance Sheet

The First Company Law Directive, issued in March 1968, stated that all limited companies and partnerships limited by shares must publish an annual balance sheet and
profit and loss account.

The proposed Fourth Directive concerning limited companies indicates:

1 The content and form of the annual accounts.
2 The rules to be employed in the valuation of assets.
3 The content both of explanatory notes to be attached to the accounts and of the management report.
4 Rules as to publicity.
5 Exemptions applicable to smaller companies.

The requirements are outlined in detail in a summary at the end of the chapter.

Capital and Dividends

The proposed Second Directive applies only to public limited companies. It lays down
rules governing the maintenance and alteration of capital, proposes a minimum paid up
share capital and restricts both the payment of dividends and the right of a company to
purchase its own shares.

Prospectus

Proposals have been made with respect to public limited companies requiring a share listing on a recognized EEC Stock Exchange either:

1 For issues in excess of 500 000 units of account (u/a), ie £200 000, or
2 For 5% of an existing quoted issue of securities of the same class.

The issuing company is required to give detailed information relating to many aspects of
its affairs including: summarized financial accounts and a funds flow statement for the
previous five years, and approved annual accounts for the last two years consolidated
where appropriate. Detailed requirements are outlined in the summary.

It is also proposed that the Stock Exchanges should have the authority to call for experts' reports on the prospectus information.

Mergers

The Third Proposed Directive only applies:

1 To mergers between public limited companies where those companies are subject to the laws and regulations of the same member state.
2 To the 'fusion' type of merger, ie where two or more companies voluntarily agree to dissolution in order that a new company can be created.

It does not, therefore, apply to the takeover bid.

The Directive attempts to safeguard the positions of all interested parties by requiring:

1 The respective managements to specify the purpose and proposed methods of the contemplated merger.
2 A report from independent experts as to the fairness of the share exchanges.

Auditing

Several Directives (eg 3rd, 4th and 5th) and a Professional Law have been proposed to deal with aspects of auditing. Between them they specify:

1 The extent, report, and qualifications needed for the undertaking of statutory audits.
2 That the auditor could be held to be liable:
    (*a*) For inaccuracies in reports or prospectuses.
    (*b*) To any interested party for inaccuracies in the annual accounts.
    (*c*) For any unfairness in share exchange dealings.
3 The rights of auditors to practise and establish a practice, in countries other than the ones in which they qualified.

Directives are also being prepared on the following matters:

1 Consolidated accounts and the regulation of integrated groups of companies.
2 Transnational mergers.
3 The regulation of insurance companies, credit institutions and finance houses.
4 Minimum educational requirements for statutory auditors including the coordination of national professional examinations and syllabus content.

It can be seen, therefore, that the proposals are extensive in scope, and are a real 'first step' along the road to harmonization.

Problems of Harmonization

The problems of harmonization may be classified in three main groups:

1   Technical (ie mainly concerned with amalgamating current practices).
2   Conceptual (ie mainly concerned with principles and general orientations).
3   Politico-cultural (ie mainly concerned with environmental influences).

Although there is a degree of overlap between them, these classifications have been presented in the order of the ascending degree of difficulty which will be experienced in order to achieve their solution.

Technical Problems

Size and organization of business units There are differences between the member states with regard to the volume of companies statutorily controlled and the size of the majority of those companies. The problem is to ascertain the minimum criteria beyond which legislation will apply, and the proposed harmonized requirements impose a minimum paid-up share capital of £10000 for the public limited company. Thus many small companies in the UK which currently enjoy limited liability will, if current proposals are accepted, be deprived of this status.

Member states have different preferences as regards their methods of raising capital. In some countries both users and providers of capital prefer debt to equity; where this is the case, capital tends to be raised on a short-term basis from institutions such as banks. Where the preference is for equity capital, it is raised on a long-term basis from private individuals as well as institutions. These preferences result in a creditor/secrecy orientation in the field of financial reporting in debt-preferring countries; and an investor/full-disclosure orientation where equity is preferred. The problem in harmonization is to develop financial reporting and disclosure practices which will satisfy both orientations.

The proposed Second Directive lays considerable emphasis on creditor protection, and is weighted towards paid-up rather than authorized share capital. It has been suggested that the Commission has chosen the creditor orientation on the basis that it is 'the orthodox procedure ruling in the majority of the member states' and not because it is likely to be 'best' practice in a developed European Economic Community.

Professionalism There are two major problems regarding harmonization of requirements for accountants. There is the need to determine minimum standards of competence, and to ascertain existing equivalents of qualification and experience. Currently, differences between member states concerning standards of competence may be summarized as:

1   There are insufficient qualified practitioners, in some countries, to provide high quality services over a wide range of activities and enterprises.
2   There is little consensus within the EEC as to the education, training and experience required before the right to practise is conferred.
3   There are differences in the status, autonomy and extent of exclusiveness granted to qualified practitioners by member states.

At least one commentator has suggested that there is no need to seek solutions to these problems because systems of training, standards and objectives are 'likely to gravitate naturally towards each other over the years'. Others take the view that attempts should be made to isolate the 'best' elements from different nations and to harmonize them into a set of European professional accounting requirements. A third approach has been suggested by the Economic and Social Committee of the EEC (ECOSOC): that the Commission should first determine what accountants are expected to do and *then* decide on the education, training and experience which will best equip them for their work.

Certainly, harmonization of professional requirements must be achieved if the EEC objective of 'free movement of labour' is to become a reality. This was a basic tenet of the original Treaty of Rome and was reiterated with regard to accountants in the proposed First Professional Law Directive.

The Commission has already begun to determine what accountants are expected to do. Under current Proposed Company Law Directives:

1 All public limited companies must have their annual accounts audited (Fourth Directive).
2 These statutory audits must include an examination of, and a report on: the books of account, annual financial statements, and the management report (Fifth Directive).
3 There must be a report on the asset valuations underlying new capital issues which are not entirely for cash (Second Directive).
4 When mergers occur, there must be a report on the fairness of share exchanges. The report must also draw a comparison between the respective companies true asset values and past and future profitability (Third Directive).
5 Stock Exchange authorities may call for a report on the validity of the information included in a prospectus (Proposed Directive on Prospectuses).

Furthermore, these proposed Directives render the auditor or report writer liable to all interested parties and for an unlimited amount, where he has acted without due care. Onus of proof as to the exercise of due care rests with the auditor or report writer.

Proposed Professional Law Directives issued by the Commission state that the work of accountants includes: bookkeeping; auditing and reporting on accounting; the rendering of opinions on the foregoing; ancillary tax advisory work; the provision of management consultancy services in connection with the foregoing.

Two factors of major importance flow from the Commission's current proposals, and are likely to create resistance to their general acceptance. Firstly, the inclusion of management consultancy work is held by some member states to jeopardize the auditor's independent position. Secondly, it is unlikely that the national professional bodies will easily accept the unlimited liability for their mistakes and misjudgements which the proposals seek to impose upon them. In June 1974, the Groupe d'Études (a study group of accountants drawn from the professional bodies of all member states) proposed that such liability should be limited. They pointed out that the prime responsibility for the accuracy of information lies with the company's management. In order to protect claimants in those cases where management cannot be held liable, the fault lying with the auditor, the Groupe d'Études proposed a system of compulsory insurance. The proposed limitation of liability would extend only to mistakes and misjudgements committed unintentionally, and not to deliberate acts.

There are also likely to be difficulties in equating qualifications and experience. In

Figure 1:4, page 16 four different attitudes to the entry requirements for full professional membership were shown to exist:

1   Only professional competence and experience are necessary (UK, Germany, Switzerland).
2   A purely academic education is sufficient (Holland, Italy).
3   Academic education and professional experience are required (Sweden).
4   Academic education and professional competence and experience, are required (Belgium, Denmark, France, Luxembourg).

There are also significant national differences in the rigour and scope of the examinations and syllabus content, and in the minimum period of experience required. It is therefore very difficult to assess objectively the equivalence of such different requirements.

At the present time, the Commission is drawing up a proposed directive which will stipulate minimum educational requirements for auditors engaged in statutory audits within the EEC. This involves:

1   Coordinating national requirements regarding admission to professional examinations and their syllabus content.
2   Formulating regulations covering persons who, although not possessing the minimum entry requirements, have been authorized to perform statutory audits (and have been doing so for some time) by the various national authorities.

Although the UK is likely to seek to shift the emphasis away from academic qualifications, it seems likely that the outcome of current discussions will be the requirement of an academic qualification of at least diploma standard.

Accounting standards Accounting standards are discussed in detail in Part II. There are two basic differences between countries caused by:

1   The relative comprehensiveness of the national statutory audit requirements.
2   The influence of tax legislation on the presentation of financial results.

The Commission's proposals regarding accounting standards are mainly to be found in the Fourth Directive. These proposals (details of which appear in the summary at the end of this chapter) relate to:

1   The structure of the annual accounts.
2   Balance sheet and profit and loss account.
3   Valuation rules.
4   Content of notes to be attached to the accounts.
5   Contents of the management report.
6   Rules as to publicity.
7   Exemptions available to smaller companies.

Overall, the concepts of 'going concern', accrual, consistency, and conservatism, will apply. Originally, it was proposed that the accounts should present as accurate a picture as possible of the company's capital, financial position and results, within the framework of the prescribed valuation rules and methods of presentation. As a result of pressure from the Groupe d'Études, the proposal now is that the prime requirement should be a 'true and fair view', even if this means departing from the suggested framework.

The Groupe d'Études has also been successful in having other suggested amendments incorporated in the revised proposed Directive:

1 That the requirement in a later Directive for consolidated accounts should be enforceable from the same date as the 4th Directive's requirements.
2 That where accelerated depreciation is charged it should be shown in the company's published accounts with any deferred taxation.

Other proposals made by the Groupe d'Études, about which a decision has not yet been made, are:

1 That the requirement in a later directive for consolidated accounts should be enforceable from the same date as the 4th Directive's requirements.
2 That exemptions from statutory audits should, for a transitional period, be available to more companies than originally proposed.

The need for the avoidance of 'contamination of accounting by tax law', stressed by both the Groupe d'Études and ECOSOC (the Economic and Social Committee of the EEC) has thus to some extent been met in the revision of the proposed 4th Directive. Omitted, to date, from the proposals issued by the Commission are any requirements for:

1 An analysis of the sources and uses of funds.
2 Information on capital employed, analysed according to location or activity.

Certain implications may be inferred from the foregoing:

1 Standards in many countries will be not merely harmonized but also raised.
2 The reported information is likely to be more meaningful as a result of the emerging emphasis on 'fair' presentation and the avoidance of the distorting tax orientation.
3 The success of the Groupe d'Études in achieving international agreement to date augurs well for future harmonization and the emergence of European standards.

Despite early British fears of conformity within a rigid and prescriptive framework, the flexibility (eg of valuation rules) which is contained within current proposals and amendments suggests that UK standards will be little affected by harmonization. It will, however, be necessary to ensure simultaneous implementation of several of the directives currently proposed.

Conceptual Problems

The major problem which emerges in this field is the lack of common, defined objectives within the Community. The search for a 'best' European system of accounting is meaningless until the decision has been made as to what purpose accounting is to serve, and which user needs are to have priority. It has been shown that different accounting practices emerge depending on whether national planning, creditor or shareholder orientations exist in a country. Currently, all of these exist within the EEC.

The second conceptual problem is the need to determine how the objectives are to be achieved, ie the nature and scope of the rules to be employed. There are currently three kinds of controls in existence within the EEC: state legislation, requirements of bodies such as Stock Exchange Councils, and professional self-regulation. The weighting given to these methods of control varies from one country to another, depending in part on the country's position on the 'developmental continuum' and in part on less tangible cultural factors.

It has been suggested in Chapter 1 that member states are already converging, in that the countries with comparatively tight legislation are introducing some flexibility into their rules, whereas the UK which has traditionally enjoyed minimum state intervention is increasing its legislation.

The third conceptual problem lies in the different national approaches to state legislation. In some countries, a prescribed uniformity of requirements exists, whereas in others only a legal framework is provided which allows considerable flexibility in practice and the exercise of professional judgement.

Politico-cultural

European harmonization, to be effective, will involve more than the mere harmonization of accounting practices and standards. Differences in attitudes and values, and national customs and strategies, will have to be accommodated if complete integration is to be achieved.

The extent to which national planning is an accepted strategy of government varies considerably between member states. In France, for example, national planning has already achieved a high degree of sophistication and general acceptance, whereas in the UK there have been few attempts to introduce an all-embracing national strategy. Where national planning is already a part of life, the implementation of a new European plan is likely to be accepted more easily than where such planning is regarded with suspicion or distaste.

In part, the extent of national planning is a reflection of different national approaches to administration. Crozier[1] shows that a cultural tendency to favour a strongly bureaucratic approach pervades most aspects of French life; he cites examples from the educational, legal and politico-administrative systems, and in the areas of industrial relations and policy-making. This 'bureaucratic phenomenon' leads to conformity based on rules, to power being wielded by formal rather than informal groups, and to a preference for dealing 'at arms length' rather than 'face to face'. This cultural tendency may be contrasted with the UK where there is a strong tradition of laissez-faire which manifests itself in a pragmatic approach to problem solving, to power often being exercised outside the formal hierarchy, and in a preference for informal 'face to face' dealing. This latter preference is perhaps outstandingly exemplified in dealings on the Stock Exchange. In a pragmatic system, changes tend to evolve gradually over time. Change in a bureaucratic system, however, resisted because of the immense ramifications it involves, tends to result from crises and explosive upheavals and is imposed from the top. It would seem that any attempt to merge two such different systems into one European administrative machine would be a daunting task.

The bureaucratic/pragmatic orientations outlined above are reflected in the respective legal systems of member countries. The bureaucratic environment results in a comprehensive set of rules enshrined in an all-embracing rigid framework. In the pragmatic UK environment, however, the approach is 'let those with the knowledge operate the controls'. This results in the development of requirements imposed by the accounting bodies on their members, by the Stock Exchange with regard to share dealings, and by the City Panel in respect of takeovers and mergers, the whole set within a flexible framework of company legislation.

These different orientations frequently result in communication and comprehension barriers. The concept of self-regulating extra-statutory bodies is difficult for the bureaucrat to comprehend; he is likely to regard them as unprincipled and tending towards the chaotic. Similarly, the concept of 'fairness' has little meaning to the bureaucrat unless the criteria are defined by legislation. An example of this comprehension barrier is seen in an article by Braun[2] in which he equates 'a true and fair view' with 'as accurately as possible', an equation which would not be made by a UK accountant.

The ease with which the cultural problems outlined above are overcome will depend in part on the amount of national pride and chauvinism which emerges during the harmonization negotiations. This factor is likely to be one of the more intractable problems. Already, a French Eurocrat has, according to Shonfield[3] stated, 'What you British will have to learn when you are in the Community is what it means to live inside a precisely defined legal system. The Community is in its very essence a system of laws.' Equal chauvinism was demonstrated by Sir Henry Benson[4] when he said that UK accounting, auditing and reporting 'is in the lead by a large margin', apparently without regard to the particular environment within which other systems exist.

Closely related to national pride is the concept of national interest. This concept is likely to be of particular importance in the harmonization of taxation policies and structures. A country's tax system is an influential element in national socio-economic strategy. A measure of harmonization of indirect taxation has been, and is continuing to be, achieved. This therefore leaves direct taxation as the main fiscal regulator in the absence of complete economic and monetary union. The distortion in financial reporting which can arise from different tax policies has already been highlighted. The sacrifice of national control implicit in the harmonization of direct taxation is unlikely to be agreed for some considerable time. The technical, conceptual and politico-cultural problems that have been outlined above indicate that full harmonization of accounting systems and practices may be a protracted process. A suggestion has been made that a pan-European form of company should be established to provide for international business needs, and a description of the proposed company follows.

The European Company

The proposed Regulation for the creation of a European company is the most extensive piece of legislation approved to date by the Commission. It contains 284 sections and an explanatory report. As well as circumventing the necessarily slow process of harmonization referred to above, the Regulation aims to stimulate European business concentration and competitiveness. It will create an alternative to the current national form of enterprise, the latter always being subject, even after harmonization, to national legislation. The trans-national European company, the Societas Europea (SE) is not intended to replace the national company; it is a proposal which will permit a specially-formed company to operate under European, as distinct from national, law. The rules governing the SE will not be allowed to diverge greatly from the proposed harmonized rules governing national companies, so that artificially created incentives and discriminations will not become the determinants of company formation. The commonality between harmonization rules and those governing the SE will tend to bolster and stimulate the proposals on both fronts. The SE will operate under European Law administered by the European Court of Justice. The form of SE is restricted to:

1   The merging of public limited companies when at least two of those companies are subject to the laws of differing member states.
2   The creation of a holding company by public limited companies in the circumstances outlined in 1 above.
3   The creation of a joint subsidiary by public limited companies in the circumstances outlined in 1 above.
4   Where an existing SE merges or creates a holding company or a joint subsidiary, with either another SE or a national public limited company.
5   The creation of an SE subsidiary by an existing SE.

Only national companies of EEC member states can participate in cases 1, 2 and 4 above, but companies registered outside the EEC can participate in cases 3 and 5. The SE is not available to private limited companies or to individuals. No national public limited company can convert into an SE. An SE may have its registered office located anywhere within the EEC, or may have more than one location, but for taxation purposes it is deemed to be located wherever the management is situated. It is proposed that an SE must have a minimum capital of 500000 u/a (£200000) if it is formed as a result of a merger or as a holding company. If it is formed as a joint subsidiary (case 3) minimum capital is 250000 u/a (£100000), and if it is a subsidiary created by an SE (case 5) 100000 u/a (£40000). The SE must be registered in a European trade register and must file with the application for registration:

1   The deed of constitution and the statutes of the founder companies.
2   The SE's regulations (memorandum and articles).
3   Its opening balance sheet and explanatory notes.
4   An auditor's report thereon, and the auditor must also report on the valuation attaching to subscriptions (other than for cash) and on guarantees that the capital will be fully subscribed.
5   The composition of the management and supervisory boards.

All the information, other than in 3, must be certified by a notary.

The proposed Regulation requires that the auditor, who is appointed by the shareholders in general meeting, must be a state authorized, professionally qualified, person entitled to conduct statutory audits of quoted public limited companies in his own member state. In addition, it contains detailed requirements covering the constitution, rights and duties of the management and supervisory boards. The provisions as to the specific qualifications and experience required of the auditor are left undefined, no doubt awaiting the proposed 'professional law' harmonization directive on minimum qualifications and reciprocity. The specific proposals concerning the auditor, management, supervisory board and shareholders' rights are similar to those contained in the proposed Fifth Company Law Directive (see Summary) for which this proposed Regulation was the model. The Regulation provides that the auditor must check that the accounting records, annual accounts, explanatory notes and the report of the management board are in accordance with the Regulation, the company's statutes and the principles of correct accounting. The text of the auditor's report is not laid down, but he must issue an unqualified report where he has no reservations concerning the annual accounts. The report of management to the shareholders must include information on:

1 The results of diversified activities.
2 Turnover of principle products and markets.
3 Changes in asset values.
4 Employee statistics and average aggregate salaries.
5 Directors' remuneration.
6 Associations with other companies.
7 Investment plans.

Accounting regulations are analagous to those prescribed by the proposed Fourth Company Law Directive, and are set out in detail in the Summary. The regulations cover the form and content of the balance sheet, profit and loss account and explanatory notes and include detailed classification and valuation requirements. Although the accounting regulations are prescriptive as to the format of financial statements and the classification rules, disclosed variations are permitted and certain alternative valuation principles are allowed. The emphasis is placed upon compliance with the valuation and classification regulations. However, within these regulations, as clear an insight as possible must be given into the assets, liabilities, finances and earnings of the enterprise. The Regulation anticipates a proposed company law directive on consolidated accounts by requiring group accounts to be prepared where appropriate. It therefore confines its provisions to stipulating the conditions in which group accounts are to be prepared, and the general principles to be followed.

The Societas Europea, because of its potential for integrating multinational interests, seems well-suited to fulfil the Treaty of Rome objectives of increased business concentration and competitiveness, and to act as a catalyst in the development of European standards of accounting, auditing and financial reporting.

Summary of Accounting and Reporting Requirements Contained in the Proposed Company Law Directives and the European Company Regulation

Accountant's Report to be Included in a Prospectus for the Sale of Securities

This proposed directive applies to public limited companies requiring a share or bond listing on a recognised EEC Stock Exchange for issues exceeding 500000 u/a (£200000), or 5% of an existing quoted issue of securities of the same class. Details must be given of:

1   The company's position in any group of companies.
2   Any of its own shares which it has purchased and whether it is allowed to do so.
3   Subsidiaries and affiliations.
4   Names of principal shareholders.
5   The nature of the company's main activities.
6   The effects of any recent mergers.
7   An analysis of turnover according to product, location and division.
8   The progress of significant new products over the last five years, the state of the market and the company's position therein.
9   Research and development expenditure and investment policies over the same period.
10   Total remuneration, including fringe benefits, paid to directors over the same period.

Financial accounts, summarized for the last five years, and a funds flow statement for the same period must be presented. Final accounts as approved by the shareholders must be presented for the last two years, consolidated accounts being required in the case of groups. Where the final approved accounts are dated more than nine months prior to the issue, a provisional unaudited statement must be submitted. The information must be presented in a prospectus conforming to a 'model' format according to the type of security being issued, the nature of the issuing institution and the type of issue operation. The Groupe d'Études has suggested that the company's auditor should report separately on the validity of the financial and accounting information, and on the profit forecasts, both reports being included in the prospectus. There are no regulations for liability of promoters for any inaccuracy.

Form and Content of Published Accounts

The main proposals concerning published accounts are contained in the proposed Fourth Company Law Directive. It contains requirements covering both public and private limited companies, the structure of their annual accounts, valuation rules, content of the notes to be attached to the accounts and contents of the management report. Annual accounts are to be filed in the appropriate registry and published in the official gazette of the member state in which the company is incorporated. The publication requirements also refer to the auditor's report and the profit appropriations where these are not shown on the face of the accounts. Where a private limited company has total assets not exceeding 100000 u/a (£40000) net turnover not exceeding 200000 u/a (£80000) and an average labour force not exceeding 20 persons during the accounting period, it need only file an abridged version of the balance sheet and is exempted from filing a profit and loss account. It must also file a statement of fixed asset movements and a note as to its profit. Those private limited companies which, although they exceed the above limits, do not exceed total assets of 1 million u/a (£400000) turnover of 2 million u/a (£800000) and 100 employees, can omit details of their turnover and trading items from their filed profit and loss account. It is proposed that individual member states may exempt these two groups of private limited companies from the publication requirements.

   The balance sheet and profit and loss account are prescribed both as to content and form in considerable detail.[5] The balance sheet may be prepared either in a vertical or horizontal form and the profit and loss account may take one of four forms: statement or account, 'natural' or 'functional'. There are provisions for minor amendments to the pre-scribed subdivisions in order to accommodate member states' particular legislation. Also, in exceptional cases, where the prescribed format would obscure the company's results and position because of the particular nature of the business, the company may adopt a more appropriate format. Some of the more significant factors concerning the format, classification and valuation of items to be shown in the accounts are outlined below.

Fixed assets These are valued basically at historic cost (acquisition or production). Production cost will include a reasonable proportion of indirect manufacturing cost. Member states may allow replacement values to be used in the case of tangible, relatively short-lived fixed assets. Methods other than replacement value 'which take into account current values' are also allowed at the discretion of member states. Periodic revaluations of tangible fixed assets are allowed. Valuation adjustments must be shown separately in the profit and loss account or the notes and shall cease to apply when the need for them no longer exists. Reserves arising from revaluation or the use of replacement cost must be shown on the equity side of the balance sheet and, when no longer required, must be writ-ten back as part of the profit and loss account result of operations for the year. Deprecia-tion must be provided regularly and systematically and any accelerations or variations in the rate of depreciation (eg for tax allowances or revaluations) should be separately dis-closed together with any relevant future taxation shown as a deduction. Fixed assets are to be shown at gross figures except where these cannot be obtained economically because of the age of the assets or lack of original records. Depreciation adjustments are shown on the equity side of the balance sheet. A statement of movements of fixed assets should be given where the information is not included on the face of the accounts.

Goodwill and intangibles Goodwill acquired for a consideration may be shown but must be written off over a period not exceeding five years. Research and development costs may be capitalized where national legislation permits it but again must be written off within five years. Other intangible fixed assets must be distinguished between those acquired for a consideration and those created by the company itself. The latter category may only appear when permitted by national legislation. Details of research and develop-ment must be shown in the directors' report.

Investments Distinction is made between equity holdings in, and claims on, associated companies. Claims on other companies in which the company has an investment must also be shown separately. For this purpose a 10% equity holding in the other company is deemed to denote an investment. Investments are to be shown at acquisition cost. Further details as to information concerning holding of at least 10% must be given in the notes to the accounts or, at least, filed in the official registry and attention drawn to this source.

Current assets and stocks The basis of valuation is that of acquisition or production cost. Allowance is made for member states to authorize exceptional valuation adjust-ments or for replacement value adjustments. The effect of these adjustments must be dis-closed either in the profit and loss account or in the notes. Adjustments in excess of current requirements must be written back. The SE Regulation specifically permits the use of 'lower of cost or market'. Stocks may be determined according to weighted average, FIFO, LIFO or some other, similar, flow method. The inclusion of overheads and general valuation rules are similar to those applicable to tangible fixed assets. Movements of current asset groups are required to be shown, as also must the method of any foreign currency translations.

Deferred charges Where national legislation permits the capitalization of deferred charges these must be written off within a maximum period of five years.

Liabilities The main differentiation is on the basis of duration of the debt (short-term, within one year; long-term, exceeding one year). Associated company obligations and debts due to companies in which there is an investment are differentiated.

Reserves and provisions Valuation adjustments (depreciation etc) are required to be shown separately. Provisions are probable or certain future expenses or losses whose exact amount or date of occurrence are uncertain. The legal reserve is obligatory in most member states but has no counterpart in Great Britain or Ireland. The reserve for own shares is equivalent to the firm's purchase of its own shares, which is shown as an asset. Statutory reserves are those required by the company's own rules. Free reserves must equal any unamortized preliminary expenses and/or research and development costs before any profit distributions can be made. No distributions can be made until capital losses have been made good. Secret reserves are specifically discouraged by the valuation rules.

Share capital The subscribed capital must be shown, with any unpaid capital shown separately as an asset. Shares of no par value are not allowed and a company cannot issue nonvoting shares in excess of one half of its subscribed capital. Bearer or registered shares may be issued. There is a minimum subscribed capital of 25 000 u/a (£10000). A company may purchase its own shares, within certain restricted proportions, and these will be shown as an asset. A reserve equal to the cost of those shares must be set up.

Accounting for acquisitions and mergers The proposed Third Company Law Directive relates to mergers between companies within the same member state and does not apply either to a takeover or acquisition or to any combination which crosses national boundaries. The implications in the proposed directive, and in the proposed Second Company Law Directive on company structure and company capital are towards full cost accounting. Further draft directives concerning integrated groups of companies, consolidated accounts and trans-national mergers are in course of preparation and will no doubt result in clearer statements of allowable practice.

Income statement In addition to the separation of the items to be classified there must be a division of turnover and profitability between products, operations and markets. Turnover is required to be net of value added tax and allowances off selling price. Details must be given of: labour force; emoluments of the board of management and supervisory board; value added tax and any other taxes on trading; compulsory and other social security costs. Non-recurring income and expenditure must be shown. Depreciation must be provided regularly and systematically. Accelerated depreciation must be separately distinguished whether as a result of taxation requirements or of permitted re-valuations. Any deferred taxation must be accounted for. Profit distributions and appropriations may be shown before or after implementation but must be included in the notes if not shown on the face of the accounts.

Other points Any financial commitments entered into which are not disclosed on the face of the accounts must be noted, as also must contingent liabilities. Comparative figures must be given. The effects of material post-date events and changes in accounting policies must be stated. In the preparation of the financial accounts the concepts of 'going concern', accrual, consistency and conservatism are to apply. The accounts are to present a 'true and fair' view of the company's capital, financial position and results, and to this end the valuation and classification rules must be secondary. Departure from the prescribed format is obligatory if fair presentation requires it.

Consolidated statements, in the form of group accounts, have been stipulated by a number of the proposed directives and the proposed SE Regulation. Thus the Proposed Directive on Prospectuses requires the production of consolidated accounts in support of information contained in a prospectus accompanying a share or bond issue. Similarly, the Regulation governing the SE requires group accounts to be prepared. However, the Commission has not yet circulated its contemplated draft proposal on the preparation of consolidated accounts, and the only specific references to date concern the occasions where consolidated accounts are required and general references to them being prepared broadly in accordance with the existing valuation and classification rules attaching to sole companies.

The proposed Fifth Company Law Directive states that an auditor must submit a written report on the results of his audit. The report must specifically refer to the following matters:

1   Whether the books of account, annual financial statements and management report conform to legal requirements and the company's own statutes.
2   Whether any infringements were discovered and, if so, their nature.
3   Whether there are in existence any facts which might seriously endanger the financial position of the company.
4   The inclusion of his certificate or short form report. This certificate must be published and is (presently) confined to stating that the financial statements, explanatory notes and management report present as accurate a picture as possible of the company's capital, financial position and results, within the framework of the prescribed valuation rules and methods of presentation. The detailed report to management need not be published. The auditor must issue a 'clean' certificate, free from qualifications, unless he has any reservations. If he has reservations he must either qualify his certificate or withhold it. There is no prescribed form of wording for his certificate.

The Groupe d'Études have suggested that the proposed directive should state that the company's annual accounts are the responsibility of the directors. The Groupe is currently attempting to limit the auditor's responsibility for the management report to those matters of a financial nature affecting and arising from the financial statements and explanatory notes. As currently proposed, the auditor's liability for damages is both unlimited and extensive and extends to creditors and customers as well as the company and individual shareholders.

The report of management (directors' report) must comment upon changes in the methods of valuation and classification used where these could distort comparisons with the previous year's figures. It must also state any material financial commitments (those to associated companies being stated separately) which are not disclosed on the face of the accounts. Names and registered addresses of those companies in which there is a capital investment of more than 10% of their equity must be stated together with details of the nature of the investment. Detail must also be given, in the case of an SE, of holdings of more than 10% of the SE's capital. In addition, the report must contain a detailed review of the company's business, its position and its likely future development. The report itself is subject to the same publication requirements as those governing the financial statements.

A Final Assessment of European Accounting Systems and Practice

It has been suggested that:

A nation's business, political and fiscal practices and public attitudes towards them, are undoubtedly more influential in determining the stage of development of the accounting profession in each of such areas than are the formal requirements of Companies Acts or professional society pronouncements. A highly developed, competent and respected public accounting profession cannot exist in a vacuum.[6]

The same may be said of accounting systems and practices. Despite the basic similarities of all European accounting systems (ie the commonality of input with double-entry bookkeeping and output with financial reports), the differences in national objectives and priorities have resulted in considerable differences in accounting systems and practices.

As the business unit has expanded in size and complexity, it has placed increasing reliance in (and onus upon) the accounting and auditing functions for control, decision-making and accountability. The recording of business transactions can still be handled adequately by means of double-entry bookkeeping; it is in the interpretation of these transactions, and in presenting them meaningfully and accurately, that the problems arise. Business transactions themselves are becoming more complex because of their longer time scale, increased inter-dependencies, and uncertainty as to possible and probable outcomes. Additionally, business transactions increasingly transcend not only industry-wide but also national boundaries. This increase in scale and complexity involves the provision of ever greater finance, resulting in the participation not only of knowledgeable and involved business promoters (as was originally the case) but also relatively uninformed, distant, private investors. Participants also include banks and other financial institutions, and Government itself to a greater or lesser extent through its taxing, incentive and intervention policies. Thus the auditor's function is tending to be prescribed by an increasingly varied assortment of individuals and institutions whose information requirements, at first sight, often appear to be mutually exclusive.

There is currently a growing recognition in Europe of the short-comings of the national systems. This recognition is manifesting itself in the proposed Nordic Companies Act (which attempts to harmonize company laws in Denmark, Finland, Norway and Sweden) and in the proposals for harmonization within the European Economic Community and for the European Company. There are also Accounting Standards Committees established at both European and international levels whose aim is to effect some commonality of published information.

Current moves in Europe represent an attempt to raise standards to a generally acceptable level, whilst permitting some flexibility of interpretation in order to cater for national and international business needs.

References

1 Crozier, M., *The Bureaucratic Phenomenon*, Tavistock, 1964, Chapters 8–10.
2 Braun, F., 'Harmonization of Company Law. The European Commission View', *The Accountant*, 1973, 169 (5153), pp 363–366.
3 Shonfield, A., 'The French Spirit and the British Intruder', Second Reith Lecture 1972, *The Listener*, 16 November 1972.
4 Benson, H., 'Harmonization of Accountancy Practice', *The Accountant*, 1972, 167 (5113), p 758.
5 For a translation by R. H. Parker of the proposed format, see *The Accountants Magazine*, 1972, 76 (789), pp 127–130.

   The UK joint professional bodies have produced an alternative 'Standard Layout of Company Accounts for EEC Company Law', published 29 July 1974 and deemed to be more suitable for use in the UK.
6 AICPA Committee on International Relations, *Professional Accounting in Twenty Five Countries*, 1964, p ix.

3

Issues of Special Concern in the Interpretation of Financial Statements

A major problem in interpreting financial statements is that the reported earnings are often unrealistic. Firstly, valuation of assets may be made meaningless by a reliance on historic cost, particularly during times of inflation. Secondly, the treatment of extraordinary items, post-date events, and associated company and consolidated earnings, all affect the significance of reported results. Thirdly, reported income may be distorted because of taxation considerations.

There are considerable variations in practice throughout Europe, but harmonization proposals to date tend to recognize, rather than attempt to resolve, the problems.

Valuation of Assets

Accounting for Inflation

Only in the UK have specific attempts been made to incorporate the effect of inflation in accounting reports. The professional accounting bodies have agreed to adopt the proposals of the Accounting Standards Steering Committee now contained in the Provisional Statement of Standard Accounting Practice Number 7, 'Accounting for changes in the purchasing power of money' issued in May 1974. The standard is not mandatory, and it is provisional pending the findings of the Sandilands Committee, set up under government auspices, to examine the effects of accounting for inflation.

The provisional standard recommends the use of a general index (based on the Retail Prices Index and using 1 January 1974 as base 100) to convert historic cost to a general purchasing power equivalent. The adjusted figures should be published in a supplementary statement annexed to the traditional historic cost financial statements. The auditor's report should cover the supplementary statement as an integral part of the notes to the financial accounts. The directors' report should explain the basis used for the preparation of the statement, and should comment on the significance of the figures. The method requires the index-adjusted values of assets to be reduced, where relevant, to the net realizable value or the 'value to the business', as appropriate. Losses or gains of purchasing power on monetary assets should be calculated and included in the supplementary statement. Depreciation charges shown in the historical cost statements are to be adjusted on the same bases as the assets to which they apply. Initially, the provisional standard is applicable only to quoted companies, although it is hoped that the larger, unquoted companies will also adopt its provisions. The standard carries no sanctions on departures from its requirements, and does not require auditors to mention any such departures in their report. Thus the situation in the UK is that some firms may produce supplementary statements of inflation-adjusted results which conform to the standard, some may produce supplementary statements without conforming to the standard, and others may not produce any supplementary statements at all.

The general index method only attempts to isolate the effect of inflation on the reported results. It precludes the use of separate indices for individual groups of assets and therefore makes no attempt to arrive at a figure representing current operating profit after allowing for technological, obsolescence, supply and/or demand factors. It merely restates the historical figures in current money terms related to general purchasing power. Thus, while the *quantity* of reported information is certainly increased, it has been argued that the *quality* of information is not necessarily improved, since the worth of a business is a function of the 'exchange values' of its assets and these 'exchange values' do not always move in sympathy with a general purchasing power index. It is, however, an attempt to formalize reporting practice, and make financial information more meaningful by recognizing that inflation does reduce the validity of reported results based upon unadjusted historic costs.

The Use of Current Values

The current value method seeks to maintain the economic substance of an enterprise. It therefore attempts to deal not only with the effect of changing price levels, but also with price variations generally, whether they are occasioned by changes in purchasing power or by changing technological, supply or demand factors.

It is used most frequently and consistently by a number of firms registered in Holland. It has been used for many years by at least one of the larger international firms and is currently practised by around 15% of Dutch quoted companies. The method is supported by the Dutch accounting profession and is recommended by the study group currently compiling an inventory of acceptable business and reporting standards. This study group is comprised of representatives of employers' organizations, trade unions and the Dutch accounting profession, and its work is analogous to that of the ASSC in the UK.

Under this method, fixed assets and stocks are continually adjusted to their current value, either by reference to current price lists or trade information, or by the application of indices specific to the particular asset or group of assets. The adjustments are incorporated in the bookkeeping records and therefore form the basis of the published accounts. The adjustments are placed to a revaluation reserve, and the bases of valuation are disclosed in a note to the financial accounts. Depreciation based on current value is distinguished from that which would have been based on cost, and for taxation purposes only the latter charge is allowable in Holland.

It is not possible, using current values, to isolate those changes brought about solely as a result of inflation, since the other variables are not constant. Furthermore, the current value method does not attempt to record losses or gains emanating from the holding of monetary assets and liabilities during times of diminishing purchasing power. Consequently, it does not necessarily show the full extent of the changes in a firm's equity over a given period. However, the method does allow a comparatively realistic assessment of the firm's current *operating* profit to be reported after the economic substance of the enterprise has been maintained.

Intermittent Asset Revaluation

In a number of European countries assets may be revalued upwards where their value has materially increased. Usually, any such increase must be part of a revaluation of the whole enterprise rather than be related to individual, selected assets or groups. The excess on a revaluation would be applied to write down other assets, to offset accumulated losses, or would be capitalized. In the UK and France, however, any excess on a revaluation can be distributed, provided that it has been realized.

Certain countries have specifically encouraged fixed asset revaluations. France allowed a series of periodic revaluations up to 1959, utilizing government-sponsored price-level indices. Both Belgium and Italy have instigated a single nation-wide revaluation, the former in 1946, the latter in 1952. In the UK and France legislation allows, and practice results in, fairly frequent revaluation (particularly in regard to land) and the depreciation charge is likely to be calculated on the increased value. In Belgium, Denmark, Italy and Sweden, revaluation is permitted by legislation in certain cases, but practice normally shows assets at cost or some lower figure. The depreciation charge in all four of these countries is restricted to the original historic cost of the revalued asset. In Holland, unless current value or an index adjustment is applied, historic cost is normally used. In Germany, Luxembourg and Switzerland, asset values are specifically precluded from exceeding historic cost.

European Harmonization Proposals

The rules currently proposed for European harmonization and the European Company do not preclude adjustments for inflation. Valuation is assumed to be based on historic cost, but current values and periodic revaluations are also permitted at the discretion of member states. Absent from current proposals is any specific reference to the application of a general purchasing power index, although use of such an index is not specifically precluded.

Treatment of Extraordinary Items

The interpretation of the current year's results, as they appear in the income statement, is influenced by the inclusion or exclusion of material items. There are inconsistencies of treatment in many instances where doubt exists as to whether exceptional and nonrecurrent items should be:

1   Charged in arriving at current net profits.
2   Placed directly to reserves without affecting current profits.
3   Referred to specifically by the auditors or directors in their reports.

Only in the UK have extraordinary items been defined. The UK profession has, in its mandatory SSAP Number 6, defined extraordinary items as those:

> Which derive from events or transactions outside the ordinary activities of the business and which are both material and expected not to recur frequently or regularly. They do not include items which, though exceptional on account of size and incidence (and which therefore may require separate disclosure), derive from the ordinary activities of the business. Neither do they include prior-year items merely because they relate to a prior year.

Examples of extraordinary items, depending on the circumstances of a particular business, are given and include:

1   The discontinuance of a significant part of a business.
2   The sale of an investment not acquired with the intention of resale.
3   The writing-off of intangibles because of unusual events or developments during the period.

Where extraordinary items exist they are required to be shown separately (less any attributable taxation) after the ordinary results of the period have been ascertained, so that results, both gross and net of extraordinary items, are distinguished.

In France, statutory requirements exist in the form of the Plan Comptable which stipulates that 'exceptional' items and prior-year adjustments must be shown and separately distinguished in the profit and loss account. Thus, a prior-year adjustment may affect the profit for the current year. There is, however, (in common with all the other continental European countries) no definition distinguishing 'extraordinary' from 'exceptional' items. Thus, a large trading loss may be 'exceptional', but because of its trading nature would not (in terms of the UK definition) be considered 'extraordinary'.

In Germany, Holland and Sweden there are statutory requirements to show 'extraordinary' items separately in the income statement. There is no separate requirement concerning prior-year adjustments.

In Denmark, there are no statutory requirements. However, as a result of the Danish profession's recommendations concerning the form and content of published accounts, best practice would treat extraordinary items and prior-year adjustments as they are treated in the UK.

In Belgium, Italy, Luxembourg and Switzerland there are no statutory requirements or professional recommendations, and consequently there is seldom any disclosure of extraordinary items.

While there is little controversy over the method required for disclosing extraordinary items (most authorities deprecating direct transfers to or from reserves as not being in the interest of full and fair disclosure), there is some concern over items which can properly be described as extraordinary. In the case of the three examples stated in the UK definition given above, it has been argued that:

1   The item arises either because of a direct decision on the part of management to curtail a business activity, or because a normal business risk undertaken has materialized to the firm's disadvantage.
2   The effect of such a decision or risk is a normal operating item and cannot properly be regarded as extraordinary.

The proposals for the harmonization of European financial statements and the European Company require that 'nonrecurrent' items should be separately shown in the income statement, but do not distinguish 'extraordinary' from other nonrecurrent items. There are no requirements concerning prior-year adjustments, and these may, therefore, under current proposals, affect the current year's profits.

Treatment of After-date Events and Similar Matters

Events sometimes occur after the period to which the financial statements relate, but are known to the company when the statements are prepared and may materially affect their interpretation. Contingent liabilities and capital commitments are similar to after-date events in the effect they may have on the interpretation of financial statements.

The degree of disclosure of these matters in financial statements varies according to national practice. In the UK and Denmark all three matters are disclosed either on the face of the accounts or by means of notes. Dutch practice discloses after-date events and contingent liabilities but does not always disclose capital commitments. Capital commitments are rarely disclosed in Sweden and never in Germany, but in both countries after-date events and contingent liabilities are shown. Italy never discloses capital commitments, sometimes shows contingent liabilities, and often draws attention to after-date events. Contingent liabilities are always disclosed in France and Switzerland, and sometimes in Belgium and Luxembourg; after-date events and capital commitments would not be shown in these four countries. The European harmonization proposals require disclosure of all three matters.

Accounting for Associated Companies

There are three aspects of accounting for associated companies which may affect the interpretation of financial statements:

1   The basis for valuing the holding in the associated company must be known. The holding may be valued on the basis of its original cost, but this may not reflect the realistic worth of the holding. Alternatively, the holding may be valued on the basis of

the investor's share of the net assets of the associated company, adjusted by any premium or discount on acquisition. This is known as the 'equity' method of valuation.

2   The basis for accounting for the earnings from the associated company should be disclosed. The earnings may be restricted to dividends received from and declared by the associated company, or alternatively the earnings may include undistributed as well as distributed profits. The latter method is used when the equity method of valuation is applied.

3   The criterion for determining when a company is to be regarded as 'associated' is difficult to stipulate. Whatever the proportion of shareholding decided upon, it is possible for the investor company to ensure that its holding remains below the stipulated proportion if it wishes to avoid disclosing its association.

The current practice in Europe is summarized in Figure 3:1.

   The European harmonization proposals do not specifically recognize the equity basis, and associated companies must be shown at acquisition cost. Details must be given of the individual names of, and the extent of interest in, any companies where the investor company holds 10% or more of the equity. Additionally, details must be disclosed of any claims by the investor company on its associates.

Consolidated Financial Statements

There are two aspects of consolidated statements which influence their interpretation: the method of incorporating individual company net assets into the group holding; and the nature and extent of information disclosed.

Incorporating Individual Company Net Assets into the Group Holding

There are three methods in use in Europe:

1   'Full cost' accounting, whereby the assets of the acquired companies are recorded at their acquisition values, purchase price being based on the market value of the shares offered as consideration. Goodwill and share premium accounts are opened; the former records the difference between net asset values and the purchase price, while the latter records the difference between the nominal value of the shares and their market value. The weakness of the method lies in the volatility of share values, which often results in a market value of dubious validity.

2   'Nominal cost' accounting, whereby the purchase price is made up of shares at par value which may or may not give rise to a goodwill account.

3   'Pooling' method, whereby the amalgamation takes place on agreed terms between the parties. The agreement may well result in the combined assets being shown at less than acquisition cost, since any goodwill arising on the combination is written off against any premium arising on the shares issued in consideration.

In the UK all three methods are practised. In 1971 the ASSC issued an Exposure Draft which differentiated merger from takeover situations, and which permitted the 'pooling' method in the former case. Attempts are currently being made to recommend a common

Key:

*signifies that use/non-use is mandatory

Country	Valuation of holding		Accounting for earnings		Definition of association	Explanatory notes
	Cost	Equity	Dividends only	Profits		
United Kingdom & Republic of Ireland	✓	✓ *		✓ *	20% + *	Departure from equity method is permitted if justified. Names of, and extent of interest in, other companies must be disclosed
Belgium	✓		✓			A list of names is usually provided, but the extent of holding is not disclosed
Denmark	✓		✓			
France	✓	✓ *	✓	*	10% + *	Must disclose net income, sales, and extent of interest in any associated companies
Germany	✓ *		✓ *		25% + *	Must disclose extent of association and any claims, liabilities and majority interests, also details of share dealings. Inclusion of foreign-domiciled associated companies is optional
Holland	✓	✓	✓	✓	25% + *	Holdings of between 15/25% require disclosure of name and domicile only. Additionally, holdings of 25% + require 'fair' values to be shown, by any method
Italy	✓		✓			
Luxembourg	✓		✓			A list of names is usually provided, but the extent of holding is not disclosed
Sweden	✓ *		✓ *			Proposed company law reforms recommend more disclosure of information
Switzerland	✓ *		✓ *			

Figure 3:1   Summary of European practice in accounting for associated companies

standard method of accounting for both merger and takeover situations.

In Italy there is no standard practice, but all methods have been used.

In Belgium, Denmark, France, Germany, Luxembourg, Sweden and Switzerland there is no standard practice, but the 'pooling' method is not recognized in any of these countries. In Germany, no distinction is made between pre- and post- acquisition profits, and therefore goodwill may fluctuate from year to year with movements on the reserves of subsidiaries. In Switzerland methods tend to be governed by factors which would maximize tax advantage.

In Holland, 'full cost' accounting is the most common method, often based on current values of assets.

The European harmonization proposals have so far dealt only with mergers within national boundaries, and they imply the recognition of only the 'full cost' accounting method.

The Nature and Extent of Information Disclosed

In the UK group accounts consisting of the consolidated balance sheet and profit and loss account and the parent company's balance sheet must be published. Additionally, the consolidated profit attributed to the parent company must be noted.

In Denmark and Holland consolidated statements, but not necessarily group accounts, must be filed. In Holland, the minimum requirement is that the statements must consist of the individual accounts of all the companies in the group, but in practice some or all of the subsidiaries are often presented in consolidated form.

In Germany a consolidated balance sheet and profit and loss account, and a group management report, must be presented for all the domestic companies in a group. Foreign subsidiaries may be included at the parent company's discretion. Details of share dealings between subsidiary companies must be disclosed in the management report.

In Sweden, there are no legal requirements for publication, but a consolidated balance sheet or a group statement must be presented to the auditor and the board, but not to shareholders. The shareholders must, however, be informed of group results, accumulated profits, free reserves, inter-company balances and the extent of the parent company holding in subsidiaries. They must also be provided with the individual subsidiaries' balance sheets.

In France, consolidated statements are not legally required but are proposed in company law reform. However, a holding company must publish the net income, sales, and parent company equity of its first tier subsidiaries. The French Stock Exchange requires consolidated accounts to be presented to it on an initial listing application only.

In Belgium, Italy, Luxembourg and Switzerland there are no statutory requirements, and therefore consolidated statements are not normally prepared. In Belgium and Luxembourg the law prohibits the use of consolidated accounts in substitution for the individual company balance sheets in certain cases. In Switzerland the Stock Exchange has recommended firms to supply consolidated statements or group accounts. Some firms in Switzerland and Italy do provide voluntarily some consolidated information.

The European harmonization proposals do not to date include any concerning consolidated statements, though the Fourth Directive refers to the need for them and there are some in preparation.

Effect of Taxation on Reported Income

In Belgium, France, Germany, Italy, Luxembourg and Switzerland legislation stipulates that business expenses, to be allowed against tax, must be charged in the published financial statements. The requirement that taxable and reported profits must coincide, often results in firms minimizing reported profits in order to mitigate tax liability. In France and Germany depreciation must be provided systematically, but in France a firm may switch from straight-line to diminishing balance depreciation in order to achieve maximum tax advantage. Any such change in policy is unlikely to be disclosed. In all these countries, accelerated depreciation is likely to be charged against reported profits where the tax legislation allows it, and depreciation is not, therefore, related to the asset's estimated useful life. The extent of any such accelerated depreciation would not be disclosed. In Sweden, although there is no requirement for tax and reported depreciation to coincide, in practice the reported profits are often reduced to a minimum commensurate with the tax allowances. However, best practice in Sweden is increasingly disclosing the amount of distortion caused to reported profits as a result of tax considerations. In Switzerland, it is quite common for the tax accrual to be less than the liability arising on the current profits, and in Italy tax liabilities are often restricted to the actual cash payments during the period, in order to preserve a firm's bargaining position. In Italy, distortions also arise when a firm capitalizes expenditure previously charged to revenue but subsequently disallowed for tax purposes.

In countries where tax legislation does not require a similarity between taxable and reported profits, there may be a considerable time lag in the charging of reported profits to tax. This time lag is likely to result in reduced cash outflows from the firm in early years, increasing over time as the tax liabilities cease to be deferred. The amounts involved can be large, and may materially overstate the reported profits unless the deferred liability is reported. In a number of countries the effect of the time lag is being increasingly recognized and disclosed. The UK currently requires that deferred taxation must be disclosed specifically in the financial statements. In Denmark, although firms are now required to account for any deferred taxation, the items need not be incorporated in the financial statements, provided that the amounts are stated in a note to the accounts. In Holland, where taxation accounting is not practised to any great extent, there is no requirement to disclose deferred tax although the use of a deferred taxation account, or a note of the amounts, is becoming increasingly common. In Sweden, accounting for deferred taxation is seldom practised, although the amount of distortion caused by tax considerations is sometimes disclosed.

The harmonization proposals do require accounting for deferred taxation. They also require companies to differentiate between 'normal' and 'accelerated' depreciation, which will therefore provide some information as to the extent of tax distortion in those countries which have traditionally required similarity between expenses allowable for tax and those charged in the financial accounts.

The Interpretation of Financial Statements

It is clear from the foregoing that the significance of financial statements is greatly affected by the items which are included in or omitted from them, and by their accounting treatment. The differences in treatment revealed in this chapter may be justifiable according to the circumstances in which the statements are compiled and their general orientation.

Many of the differences would disappear if agreement could be reached on:

1   The purposes of external reporting – ie whether financial statements should reflect the efficiency of the enterprise from the economic point of view or whether they should be orientated towards external users of information.
2   The identification of the users of accounting information and their needs.

Once agreement on these points is reached, agreement on the statements' orientation would follow.

Part 2

National Surveys

4

The United Kingdom and Republic of Ireland

Type of Business Unit

Companies with Limited Liability

Such companies are controlled, in the UK, by the provisions of the Companies Acts 1948 and 1967 (1960 for N Ireland; 1963 for the Republic). These companies are almost entirely limited by shares (although a few are limited by guarantee) and are comprised of:

1   Public companies with unlimited right of share transfer, at least two directors appointed by the shareholders, and published annual audited accounts together with (unaudited) directors' report and annual return.
2   Private companies which restrict the right of share transfer, limit the number of members, need have only one director, and must file – but not necessarily publish – annual audited accounts.

Corporations Based on Statutory Instruments etc

Certain corporations are brought into existence by means of Statutory Instruments, eg nationalized undertakings, public utilities etc and others have been formed by Royal Charter, but as the rules governing such organizations tend to be specific to the individual organization rather than nationally determined they are beyond the scope of this survey.

Partnerships

Even where a partnership is classed as limited, and this is rare, there must be at least one unlimited partner. They are governed by the Partnership Act 1890 and Limited Partnerships Act 1907 respectively, as amended by the Companies Act 1967 as to maximum number of partners. Where such number exceeds 50 – 20 in the case of a partnership in banking – the partnership must register as a company.

Sole trader with unlimited liability

Branches of Foreign Corporations

A branch of a foreign corporation can be set up subject to Treasury approval. Such a branch must file the name of a UK resident in whose name the company can be sued, and also copies of the company's certificate of incorporation or charter, rules and directors' particulars. Copies of the company's annual accounts, prepared broadly in accordance with the terms of the Companies Acts, must also be filed.

Business Records

Companies are required to keep proper books of account showing, *inter alia*, all amounts received and expended, sales and purchases of goods, and assets and liabilities. Registers of share- and debenture-holders, directors and secretary, and loans to the company, must also be kept. In addition, such books must be kept in a manner sufficient to give a true and fair view of the company's affairs and to explain its transactions.

The Accounting Profession

Basically, professionalism in accounting stems firstly from the Joint Stock Companies Acts, of 1844 (which required annual appointment of auditors) and 1856 (which allowed the appointment of an auditor who was not himself a shareholder, and also permitted him to employ persons to conduct an audit at company expense). Secondly, there are the Chartered Institutes: in Scotland, dating from 1854 and in England and Wales from 1880. These Chartered Institutes, together with that in Ireland and the Association of Certified Accountants, are currently recognized by the Department of Trade and Industry for the purpose of conducting limited company audits. Outside this recognition, because of their self-evident specialisms, are the Institute of Cost and Management Accountants and the Chartered Institute of Public Finance and Accountancy. A person who wishes to audit public company accounts must, therefore, be a member of one of the four recognized bodies.

Currently, the number of accountants engaged in public practice is approximately 25000 practising in partnership form or as sole practitioners, as they are not allowed to form limited liability companies for audit work. They audit 3300 quoted public limited companies in the UK with a total market capitalization of £50000 million as well as numerous private limited companies.

Qualifications required for membership of the bodies are basically similar, although those for the Institute of Chartered Accountants in England and Wales (ICAEW) will be described since it is through this body that the majority of accountants qualify. Recruits to the profession must possess certain basic educational qualifications, not necessarily relevant to accounting. The training period of three or four years (the length of which is determined by the recruit's existing qualifications) is a purely practical one and must be undertaken within a practitioner's office. During – and again at the end of – the training period, the recruit is required to pass a set of examinations which are narrowly vocational in scope, and which are set and supervised by the Institute. The subject matter of the examinations relates solely to the practical rather than the theoretical aspects of accounting. The training and examinations are concerned with current practice and procedures, little consideration being given to examining weaknesses in current practice nor to likely or desirable future developments. Admittance to membership of the Institute is dependent upon the satisfactory completion of the examinations and training contract. The earliest age at which a recruit can be admitted is 22 years. Currently, attempts are being made to raise minimum entry requirements, and to encourage the acquisition of a sound theoretical base to support the practical training. Recently, graduates in 'relevant' subjects have been exempted from the initial set of examinations, and attempts are being made to attract more graduates into the profession. It is anticipated that some period of post-qualification experience will be required before a member is permitted to practise. A further attempt to raise current standards is seen in the proposals for post-qualification examinations, (successful completion of which will be required before a Fellowship of the Institute is granted) and in the Solomons Report on the future education and training of professional accountants.[1]

In addition to conducting audits and reporting on the financial statements of enterprises, the accountant in public practice also undertakes taxation and management advisory work on behalf of his clients and may undertake special investigations for both company and government purposes. He may also act as liquidator, receiver or trustee in bankruptcy, company secretary or registrar, and is often involved in the valuation of shares for various purposes. The UK accountant, therefore, undertakes a wide range of duties, some of which tend to throw in doubt his independence as an auditor but which demonstrate his high status in the country at large. He is governed by a rigorous set of professional ethics, although these are not set down as an official code, and breach of these will result in professional disciplinary action or expulsion from his Institute.

Statutory Requirements

The Companies Acts are the major statutes controlling accounting and reporting, and they are systematically and periodically revised by a committee which is appointed on an ad hoc basis, which derives its recommendations largely from expert testimony and appropriate papers submitted by interested professional organizations. Up to the present time, such Acts have been passed at approximately twenty year intervals, although the current changes in the business environment are such that a new Companies Act is likely to be introduced in the very near future, within a decade of the passing of the last Companies Act (see Current Trends later in this chapter). The committees considering company law reform include, as a matter of course, both company and public accountants, and consequently a pragmatic approach can be discerned. The influence of actual business practices is paramount, the legislation is relatively current and, in general, wide latitude in the choice of actual accounting practice is allowed.

To date the accounting function has been seen as the need to give 'a true and fair view', the choice of individual practice being subordinated to its consistent application and its appropriate reflection of the circumstances. The comparative frequency of new Companies Acts has meant in some instances that the legal requirements have actually led the development process of accounting, although in most cases they have tended to formalize the best practices currently in use. There will no doubt always be some accountants who regard current legislation as a ceiling of acceptable practice whereas others will view it as an enforcement of minimum standards only. Nevertheless, the Companies Acts – dealing in the main with the auditor, balance sheet, profit and loss account, consolidations, prospectuses and dissolutions – do provide a useful chronicle of the nature of the development of the UK system of accounting. Furthermore, a number of the enactments can be seen as attempts to impose statutory sanctions in order to strengthen the position of the auditor in following the best professional practice at such times.

The principal areas governed by current Companies legislation concern the filing and publication of company information, including: prospectus; Memorandum and Articles of Association; annual audited balance sheet and profit & loss account; and auditor's and directors' reports to the shareholders. Details of the legal requirements are included in the overall summary of current UK practice given on Page 64.

Standards

Auditing

Professional audit standards are not defined by law but, traditionally, have been promulgated in general form by the ICAs and the Association of Certified Accountants (ACA) The emphasis has been on the individual auditor using those standards which, in his opinion, are necessary:

1   For the presentation of a 'true and fair view' of the state of a company's affairs.
2   To ensure compliance with the Companies Acts.

Statements have been issued by the ICAEW periodically on: general principles (1961), internal control (1964), auditors' reports on group accounts (1965), confirmation of debtor balances (1965), stocktaking (attendance, 1968, general, 1969), auditors' reports (1968), working papers (1969), statements of standard accounting practice on auditors' reports (1971), etc.

The independence of auditors is stressed in the general principles statement (1961) which states:

Auditors have their own independent responsibility to form and express their professional opinion on the accounts to be presented by the directors to the shareholders. . . They must approach their work as auditors with an independent outlook and must do nothing which would impair that independence.

Reporting

Auditors must state expressly whether in their opinion the accounts on which they are reporting give a true and fair view and have been properly prepared in accordance with the provisions of the Companies Acts 1948 and 1967. If they are unable to report affirmatively in the required respects they must say so. Additionally, they are required to form an opinion as to whether proper books of account have been kept by the company, proper and adequate returns have been made by branches not visited, if applicable, and the accounts are in agreement with the books of account and returns. The absence of specific comment on the above implies that the auditor has satisfactorily investigated and satisfied himself on these matters. The auditor must also include any facts required by the Companies Acts to be stated in the accounts or in notes thereto, and which have been omitted.

The board of directors must also report to the members annually with the presentation of the audited accounts. Such report must contain particulars of the amount of any proposed dividends and appropriations to or from reserves, and also any material change in the nature of the company's business or interests. Such a directors' report is not specifically reported on by the auditor, whose duties are confined to the accounts and the notes attached thereto.

Accounting

In general, accounting standards up to the end of the 1960s have taken the form of 'Recommendations on Accounting Principles' published by the professional bodies to provide direction and guidance for their members within the general framework of the Companies Acts. These recommendations were not binding on members, and depended for recognition on being generally accepted by the business community. However, in December 1969 the ICAEW issued a 'Statement of Intent on Accounting Standards in the 1970s' with the following main aims:

1 The narrowing of differences and variety in accounting practice.
2 The disclosure of accounting bases.
3 The disclosure of departure from established definitive Accounting Standards.

Accordingly, the Accounting Standards Steering Committee (ASSC) was formed which is now comprised of members of the professional accounting bodies together with liaison members from industry, issuing houses, analysts, the Stock Exchange, and the City Panel on Takeovers and Mergers. The ASSC publishes exposure drafts of the proposed new standards and then, following public representation, the final draft is published subject to the approval of the Councils of the professional accounting bodies, as a definitive 'Statement of Standard Accounting Practice'. Although the Statements do not outline 'the only' correct treatment, they are intended to indicate the alternatives which should be adopted in the interests of conformity and comparability. Any departure from a Standard Accounting Practice which is not disclosed and explained may be investigated by the Councils of the Institutes. To date, the following Statements have been issued:

1 Accounting for the results of associated companies (January 1971; revised August 1974).

2   Disclosure of accounting policies (November 1971).
3   Earnings per share (February 1972; revised August 1974).
4   The accounting treatment of Government grants (April 1974).
5   Accounting for Value Added Tax (April 1974).
6   Extraordinary items and prior-year adjustments (April 1974).
7   Accounting for changes in the purchasing power of money (May 1974). Provisional statement only.
8   The treatment of taxation under the imputation system in the accounts of companies (August 1974).

Exposure Drafts which have been issued but which are still awaiting adoption as definitive Standards are as follows:

3   Accounting for acquisitions and mergers (January 1971).
6   Stocks and work in progress (May 1972).
11 Accounting for deferred taxation (May 1973).
13 Statements of source and application of funds (April 1974).
14 Accounting for research and development (January 1975).
15 Accounting for depreciation (January 1975).

To date, further draft Statements are proposed on the following matters:

Form and content of group accounts.
Accounting for diversified operations.

In addition to the Statutory requirements and those determined by the Statements of Standard Accounting Practice, there are other common practices which have evolved over time. Some of these are buttressed, or have been initiated, by the requirements of extra-statutory bodies such as the Stock Exchange and the City Panel on Takeovers and Mergers.

Extra-statutory Requirements

There are three principal sources of extra-statutory requirements concerning the financial reporting and disclosure practices of UK limited companies. These are: the professional accounting bodies; the Stock Exchange Council; and the City Panel on Takeovers and Mergers. The accent throughout has been on the self-regulatory function of accounting and business generally, and also on the potential advantages accruing from a system which has a considerable amount of flexibility. This flexibility permits a responsiveness to changing conditions, while, at the same time, incorporating a process of judgement, sanction and exposure imposed by professional peers. The extra-statutory requirements currently in operation may be summarised as follows:

Professional Bodies

Apart from the disciplinary committees of the various professional accountancy bodies, the main contribution in this area is the on-going work of the Accounting Standards

Steering Committee. The Statements of Standard Accounting Practice are intended to be both definitive and mandatory.

Stock Exchange

In general, the Council of the Stock Exchange has evolved its requirements regarding both financial reporting, and listing and prospectuses, within the framework of the Companies Acts. In most instances the Council's requirements supplement the current Companies Act, often being adopted to some degree in a subsequent Act.

Financial reporting requirements The Stock Exchange requires half-yearly reports from listed companies – under penalty of withdrawal of permission to deal in that company's shares – on: profits and losses; proportion of profits attributable to the holding company, if applicable; details of taxation charges, both domestic and overseas; the effect on profits of any extraordinary items; the rates of dividends proposed and paid; and any other material information relevant to an appreciation of the results. Such reports are not required to be audited but relevant comparative figures must be provided. It is presumed, subject to any information to the contrary, that normal statutory and accounting standards (eg consolidated results, asset valuations, depreciation, consistency, etc) have been complied with in ascertaining those results. There are also requirements as to the communication of events both to the Stock Exchange and the general public.

Listing requirements and prospectuses As well as the statutory information to be included in a prospectus, the Stock Exchange requires an accountant's report where there has been a previous quotation. In order to protect existing shareholders, the company must undertake that first options to subscribe to any subsequent rights issues must be given to them. Finally, companies seeking a listing on the Stock Exchange must expect a market capitalization of at least £500 000 in total, and £200 000 for any one security.

City Panel on Takeovers and Mergers

Created in Spring 1969, as a semi-private panel, the City Panel on Takeovers and Mergers was an attempt to preserve the traditional right of the City to discipline itself and to avert the introduction of a British equivalent of the American Securities and Exchange Commission. The Panel was formed by the Bank of England, representatives of the major financial institutions and the Stock Exchange, and has the implied backing of the Department of Trade and Industry which is the ultimate authority. The Panel's duty is seen to be the enforcement of good business standards, rather than of law, in an attempt to reconcile the needs of both speed and justice in takeover transactions. The Panel has adapted and revised the 'City Code' originally promulgated under the auspices of the Bank of England, and this now falls into two categories:

1 General principles of conduct to be observed in bid situations.
2 A set of rules applicable to dealing.

The principles and most of the rules are imprecise – and deliberately so – in order to allow for discussion, interpretation and flexibility. They have subsequently been reissued, in revised form, in February 1972 and again in June 1974. The City Panel's Code places great emphasis on companies conforming to the spirit (as well as the letter) of the principles and rules, and embraces dealings in the shares of unquoted and private companies as well as quoted companies. The principles are generally concerned with protecting shareholders in a bid situation by ensuring that they have full information, that the offer is bona fide and not intended to create a false market, that shareholders of a particular class are treated equally, and that minorities are treated fairly. The interests of the directors must be subjugated to those of the shareholders, employees and creditors. The rules are concerned with every aspect of a potential takeover or merger.

To a considerable extent the three sources of extra-statutory requirements outlined above tend to support one another, although the most powerful of the three – from the point of view of the sanctions it can impose – is probably the Stock Exchange. This sanction, the threat of withdrawal of permission to deal, provides a strong incentive to directors and reporting accountants to conform to the Stock Exchange requirements. At the same time it provides both a disciplinary force and a source of authority to the auditor in any situation where he is in conflict with the directors. It is the threat of action by the City Panel to persuade the Stock Exchange to prohibit dealing in a particular share, or to refer the case to the Department of Trade and Industry for investigation, that disciplines companies involved in takeovers and mergers. The SSAPs being issued by the Standards Steering Committee have much more impact because they are approved and authorized by the Stock Exchange in its financial reporting requirements. Despite its potential, the City Panel is weakened by its requiring discipline by general agreement. It has been stated that it does not possess any attribute of independence of constitution, and is very much a 'one man show' because of the power wielded by its Director-General. However, since it has succeeded to date in averting the introduction of a British Securities and Exchange Commission on American lines and since its brief was to preserve the traditional right of the City to impose its own discipline, it must be judged as having been successful.

Summary of the Principal Areas of Current Accounting and Reporting Requirements in the UK and the Republic of Ireland

Accountant's Report to be Included in a Prospectus for the Sale of Securities

Current profits, losses, assets and liabilities must be shown and an analysis of profits and losses for the immediately preceding five years must be given. Such an analysis must explain profit trends (including the effect of any asset and structural changes) and include balance sheet summaries. Rates of dividends paid in the previous five years and details of the past year's and current aggregate of directors' remuneration must be given. The directors must issue a statement regarding the provision of working capital and a separate statement outlining the future prospects of the company. The accountant must comment on the accounting bases used in these statements, and withhold his signature to the formal report if he considers that the forecasts and assumptions are misleading.

Form and Content of Published Accounts

All limited liability companies, both public and private, must file Annual Returns with the Registrar of Companies within two days after the annual general meeting. Such a Return must indicate the address of the company's registered office, a summary of its authorized and issued capital, and its total indebtedness where such debts are secured. It must also include details of changes in members, shareholdings, and directors' and secretary's particulars. There must be attached to the Return copies of the audited balance sheet, profit and loss account and auditor's and directors' reports. Copies of the accounts and reports must be sent to every member and debenture holder of the company at least twenty-one days before the date of the annual general meeting.

The balance sheet must show fixed assets under separate headings with details of acquisitions and disposals during the year and a note of any shortfall between recorded and realizable values. Details must also be given of current assets; assets which are neither fixed nor current; land held; loans, other than from banks; separately classified reserves, including taxation reserves; redeemable shares and redeemed debentures available for reissue.

The profit and loss account must state the amount of turnover, where it exceeds £50000, and a description of the method by which it is calculated. Details must be given of directors' remuneration, including the Chairman's emoluments, the numbers of directors whose remuneration lies within each category of ascending bands of £2500 intervals, pensions and compensation for loss of office of directors and past directors. The number of employees whose remuneration lies within each ascending £2500 interval above £10000 must also be stated. In addition, expenditure on plant hire, depreciation, corporation tax, loan interest, income from quoted and unquoted investments, and income from land, must all be separately shown. The net amount of dividends paid and proposed, and appropriations generally, must also be shown.

Consolidated statements, in the form of group accounts must be prepared, except in very restricted cases. These accounts consist of a consolidated balance sheet and a consolidated profit and loss account, the balance sheet of the parent company and a note of the consolidated profit directly attributable to the parent company. Where there are unconsolidated subsidiaries, the reasons for non-grouping, the net aggregate amount of those subsidiaries' profits/losses attributable to the group for both the current and earlier years, and the investment in and net indebtedness of such subsidiaries, must be given. Substantially similar information is required in respect of the results of associated companies where the association is considered to be a material fact or where the investing company possesses at least 20% of the voting rights.

The detailed disclosures regarding turnover, specific remuneration and numbers of persons whose remuneration falls within specified limits, number of employees and political and charitable donations are features of the 1967 UK Companies Act but are not yet required by Irish legislation. The Republic of Ireland does not require consolidated accounts in the case of private holding companies and their subsidiaries.

The auditor's report is presented in short form only and expresses an opinion on the true and fair view of the company's affairs and its results for the period as presented by the financial statements. In addition, the auditor must say whether, in his opinion, such statements have been prepared in accordance with the requirements of the Companies Acts, whether proper books of account have been kept, and adequate returns made, and whether the accounts are in agreement with such books and returns. The auditor must state any facts which are required by the Companies Acts to be stated in the accounts or notes and which have been omitted.

The directors must also report to the members on the presentation of the annual accounts. Their report must give details of any material changes in the fixed assets of the company or its subsidiaries; the market value of assets which differ significantly from book values; the reasons for any new share or debenture issues, the number issued and the consideration received for them; directors' share acquisitions; significant contracts entered into by the company; the material classes of business carried on by the company, and the allocation of turnover and profits/losses between such classes. Where total turnover exceeds £50000 the value of goods exported must be stated and, in those companies whose British payroll normally consists of more than 100 persons, the average number employed each week. In addition, political and charitable donations in excess of a total figure of £50, any recommended dividend, and amounts carried to reserves must be shown.

Current Practice

Fixed assets These are valued basically at historical cost but have (relatively) frequent appreciation to current values because of the rise in land prices. Any increase in value is taken to capital reserve and is not available (generally) for distribution. It is recommended that provision should be made for deferred taxation on gain but a number of property companies seem to be ignoring this. The basis of gross figure (cost or valuation) is disclosed. Depreciation on higher value should be charged although this is not allowable for tax purposes. Depreciation on buildings is not always provided. Figures are shown at gross cost or valuation less accumulated depreciation. It is proposed that the values as adjusted by price level index should be shown.

Goodwill and intangibles Goodwill may be retained or written off against either profits or reserves. Goodwill arising on an acquisition may be similarly written off. Any write off will be disclosed in the analysis of movements in reserves. Intangibles with a specific life are written off over such life.

Investments These should be distinguished between quoted and unquoted. The market value of the former should be noted and so should any excess of cost over realizable value in the case of the latter.

Current assets and stocks Where asset value in realizable terms is below the figure shown this should be noted. Loans to directors, officers, etc, are normally prohibited. Stocks are valued at historical cost less any amounts written off to reduce to net realizable value or replacement price if this is lower. Such adjustments may be made on individual items, on groups or in the aggregate. The method of determining cost according to flow is not usually disclosed, although any consistently applied method is permitted (the LIFO method is not allowable for tax purposes). FIFO or average is probably the most frequently used method. Overheads are usually included in cost but need not be, and the fact is not usually disclosed. It is proposed that the value as adjusted by price level index should be shown.

Deferred charges Discount on debentures is usually written off to revenue reserves when incurred or amortized over the life of the debt. Formation expenses may, and usually are, written off over a short (five year) period.

Liabilities Distinction is made between those of short- and long-term maturity, secured or unsecured. Long-term commitments (eg long leases, etc) are not usually noted.

Reserves and provisions Distinction is made between provisions (charged against profits) and reserves (appropriations). Provisions are made for known liabilities of uncertain amounts and are normally deducted from relevant asset. Reserves may be specifically non-distributable as income (share premium, capital reserves), others may be for specific redemption or equalization purposes. Secret reserves are explicitly prohibited and, in particular, excessive amounts of depreciation set aside for tax or replacement purposes have to be identified as reserves.

Share capital Shares are shown at par or paid up value if below par, premiums on shares are shown in separate reserve. No-par value shares are prohibited. Bearer shares are not issued by UK companies. Shareholders' equity is shown as a sub-total and a company is not permitted to purchase its own shares. Bonus issues are made at par value out of either distributable or non-distributable reserves. Details of any options on shares must be stated. Dividends shown on annual accounts are proposed and require shareholder approval.

Accounting for acquisitions and mergers Practice has distinguished between full cost accounting for acquisitions and nominal value accounting for mergers in many cases, although currently, the participants or dominant party are able to define whether they have acquired or merged. The nominal value method approximates to pooling of interests.

Income statement Turnover is shown although the cost of sales and gross profits according to differentiated products, groups, activity, need not be stated. It is proposed that sales shall be noted net of VAT. Depreciation must be specifically shown and in its absence the reason for it must be stated. It is usual to provide for depreciation by the straight-line or reducing balance method, although only recently has the method been identified in the notes. Accelerated depreciation allowed for tax purposes is not normally charged in the financial accounts. Additional depreciation for obsolescence, replacement cost increases etc is normally shown as appropriations. Directors' remuneration is shown with distinction made between fees, other emoluments and pension contributions, remuneration to holding company directors from subsidiaries, and numbers of directors and employees within specified remuneration 'bands'. Charges for interest on fixed loans and amounts set aside for diminution in value of assets must be shown, as also must any income or loss from subsidiaries. Extraordinary and non-recurrent items must be shown, if material, with the calculated effect on a previous year's results of any change in an accounting base. Standards concerning prior year adjustments are currently under consideration.

Taxation accounting is not practised in UK accounts and consequently considerable differences can arise between tax as computed on profits and actual liability. The amount of UK tax on the profits as shown should be charged together with an explanation of the basis of computation and a deferred taxation or tax equalization account, employed for material differences. Rules for Government grants and VAT are also now standardized. Appropriations should be shown separately from profit determination and individually distinguished. Where applicable a separate statement showing movements on reserves must be made. Dividends paid or proposed are to be shown net of income tax.

Other points Notes as to earnings per share, calculated in accordance with standard accounting practice, and accounting policies are to be given, together with disclosure where generally accepted accounting principles based on going-concern, matching, consistency and prudence have not been followed. Comparative figures must also be shown together with the disclosure of material post-date events.

Current Trends

Attempts are currently being made to make reporting and disclosure practices within the UK 'truer' and/or 'fairer' and 'fuller'. Although these attempts coincide with Britain's entry into the European Economic Community and may be influenced by continental practice generally, most of the moves emanate from a change in the 'climate' of the business environment. Increasingly, the social and ethical responsibilities of business are being questioned, as are the effectiveness and efficiency of the various systems of voluntary control operating under the principles of 'enlightened self-interest'. These trends are evidenced by the calls for a British commission on the lines of the American Securities and Exchange Commission to strengthen current extra-statutory controls, and in the questioning of the adequacy of current accounting and auditing practices.

Statutory Trends

Both the Conservative and Labour political administrations have, within the last year, moved to promote legislation towards company law reform. In December 1973 the Conservative Government introduced a Companies Bill to Parliament but this lapsed when the February General Election was called. Shortly after the Labour administration was formed, a Green Paper was published on the same matter.[2] Broadly speaking, the two sets of proposals cover similar ground although, naturally, they differ in the emphasis given to particular aspects.

The moves for statutory reform adopt a two-part approach: there are attempts to update and amend the 1967 Act, and to formalize and amend the powers and responsibilities of the corporate organization. Briefly, the proposals aim to increase the amount of legislative control over matters which have previously been self-regulatory, and include: directors' dealings and contracts; fuller disclosure of manpower policies and employee statistics; 'insider' dealings and nominee holdings; extension of investigatory powers; and ensuring compliance with the time limits for the filing and publication of information. Attempts are also being made to distinguish 'stewardship' and 'proprietary' companies, the former being those in which ownership is divorced from control and the latter referring to companies where ownership and control are in the same hands.

The Green Paper envisages the setting up of a Companies Commission, a quasi-legislative body on the lines of the US Securities and Exchange Commission, to control

Stock Exchange activities, financial institutions and the Panel on Takeovers and Mergers. In addition, the Paper contains proposals to establish employee or trade union representation at management level, and generally requires information to be included in the directors' annual report concerning the company's relationship with the community at large. This report would be subject to audit.

The proposals can be seen as attempts to outline the 'climate' within which business must operate. They represent a 'declaration of intent' as to the orientation that business generally must use in setting its targets, determining its responsibilities and formulating its practices.

Professional Trends

Accounting standards are being criticized because:

1 They are based on inadequate legal requirements.
2 They have no agreed overall objectives.
3 They fail to ensure the independence of the auditor.
4 They do not result in the presentation of meaningful information.

In the field of auditing, criticisms have been made concerning the auditor's obsession with legal obligations, reluctance to develop ethical principles as against technical rules, and his over-emphasis on limiting his liability rather than providing information for the shareholder. Calls are being made for audit reports on management efficiency, for social audits, and for a strengthening of the auditor's independent authority. The auditor's position is hardly likely to be strengthened as a result of the ASSC's Standard on accounting for price level changes. Since the Government announced its intention to conduct an investigation into the whole question of the effect of inflation, the professional bodies have adopted an SSAP which lacks any sanctions and departure from it need not be disclosed.

Other Trends

Stock Exchange controls have tended to come under greater scrutiny because an active stock market has led to increased takeover and merger dealings and greater insecurity for management and directors generally. Resulting pressures to show results in the best possible terms tend to grow in such a climate of insecurity, and a prevailing shortage of stocks on the market assists in the inflation of share prices. It has also been suggested that the Stock Exchange fails to obtain for investors the quality and quantity of information required from quoted companies, both in published accounts and prospectuses.

There has been debate regarding the City Panel on Takeovers and Mergers centring on whether a statutorily constituted body, on the lines of the American SEC, would exercise more effective control. Proponents of the voluntary approach emphasize the advantage of the current flexibility of approach which is not likely to exist in a statutory system. Opponents,[3] however, dispute its continuing effectiveness on the grounds that it is 'only limping sadly behind events . . . it has left too large a field free to the enterprizing buccaneer'. They say it has gone as far as it can in establishing precedents and that attempts at increased codification are tending not only to obscure the spirit behind the code but also to create ambiguities and anomolies; they also see a 'basic conflict between, on

the one hand, an "unfettered market" (because market operations are covert and sectional) and, on the other, accepted takeover procedures (which are overt and democratic).'
Perhaps the most telling arguments against the City Panel will eventually turn out to be:

1   Its demonstrated need to enlist statutory backing for dealing with insiders.
2   Its inability to take a wide view – which the current proposals for company law reform imply is necessary.
3   Its apparent lack of independence from its constituent members, and the lack of publicity and sanctions available to the Panel in dealing with potential abusers of the Code.

Briston[4] states that 'the traditional secrecy of the City is an anachronism', and that 'the activities of the City must be open to public inspection and regulation so that justice is seen to be done'. He suggests that a government commission of inquiry into the role of the publicly-quoted company within the economy, and into the regulation of the activities of companies and capital markets, would find it 'absolutely necessary to have a totally independent body applying the regulations and guidelines'.

A move towards a statute-backed authority of this kind would probably have been impossible in the comparatively nonlegalistic business climate which prevailed even as recently as ten years ago. Today, society is increasingly accepting legal 'interference' in business affairs (eg Industrial Training Act 1964; Redundancy Payments Act 1965; Race Relations Act 1968; Equal Pay Act 1970). Current proposals are therefore much more in keeping with developing cultural attitudes.

The system of financial accounting as currently operated within the UK is an archetype of the 'pragmatic' approach identified by Mueller and described in the Introduction. It is noticeably lacking in any theoretical foundation and relies for its authority on the use of a few well-tried and useful 'ground-rules' or concepts, developed over time and supported by an authoritative, well-regarded, self-disciplining profession.

References

1   Solomons, D., et al, 'Prospectus for a Profession', Advisory Board for Accountancy Education, London, 1974.
2   'The Community and the Company. Reform of Company Law', Labour Party Industrial Policy Sub-committee, London, 1974.
3   See articles by Sanderson, V., 'Goodbye to Greybeards and Toothless Watchdogs', The Sunday Times, 29 April 1973; Gillum, J., 'Some New Rules for the City Code', The Times, 16 July 1973.
4   Briston, R., reported in Accountancy Age, 1973, Vol. 4, No. 27, p16.

5

Belgium

Type of Business Unit

Companies with Limited Liability

These companies are controlled by the Commercial Code which bears a marked similarity to that of France, from which it was derived. Under the limited liability heading are:

1 Public companies (Société Anonyme – SA) which have at least seven shareholders, a maximum (but renewable) life of 30 years, and transferability of shares. There must be a board of directors numbering at least three who need not be shareholders. Audited annual accounts must be filed and published together with the audited directors' report.
2 Private companies (Société de Personnes à Responsabilité Limitée – SPRL) which have between two and fifty members, a maximum (renewable) 30 year life, minimum capital of B Fr 250000 (approximately £2700), minimum share value of B Fr 1000 (£11) and restricted transferability of shares. Where the number of shareholders exceeds five a statutory examiner must be appointed. Accounts must be audited annually and filed. Any SPRL with ten members or less and a capital not exceeding B Fr 3 million (£33000) may choose to be taxed as a corporation or its members may be taxed as individuals. The form of SPRL is not permitted in insurance, banking, mortgage or stockbroking businesses.

Cooperatives

Cooperatives are rare but may be carried on under the heading of Societé Cooperative.

Such an enterprise must register and file accounts with the Registrar of Commerce, and may be an Association Momentanee (AM) of a temporary nature, or an Association Commerciale en Participation (A CEN P) such as a joint venture.

Partnerships

Partnerships may be:

1 General (Société en Nom Collectif – SEN NC), all partners have joint and several liability and at least one partner's name appears in the firm name.
2 Limited (Société en Commandite Simple – SENCS) this is the usual form with at least one general partner. Annual accounts must be filed.
3 Limited with shares (Société en Commandite Par Actions – SCA) which is becoming increasingly rare. Unlimited liability attaches to the general partners, of whom there must be at least one, while the shareholders have limited liability and transferable interests. The company laws apply to such an organization and at least three statutory examiners must be appointed. Annual accounts must be published.

Sole Traders with Unlimited Liability

Branches of Foreign Corporations

A branch of a foreign corporation may be established but it is not recognized as a separate legal entity under Belgian law. The foreign corporation's statutes and annual accounts must be published and there must be a Belgian person or enterprise appointed to be responsible for due payment of taxes.

Business Records

The Commercial Code requires the keeping of a stamped and prenumbered official journal, and a balances or inventory book, together with a share register. In addition, tax and labour legislation requires the use of stamped and approved records of sales, purchases and personnel.

The Accounting Profession

The accounting profession in Belgium is basically divided, as in France and Italy, between the auditing and accounting functions. The auditing profession is governed by the Institut des Réviseurs de Banque (IRB) and the Institut des Réviseurs d'Enterprises (IRE), the titles attaching to members of either body being protected by law. The former body is older, dating from 1935, and is regarded as the premier of the two Institutes. However, its members specialize in the fields of banking and insurance, although they may be appointed as a réviseur d'enterprises. Appointment has to be made by the Banking Commission and currently membership of the Institute is less than 50 members.

Members of the IRE, therefore, are primarily involved in the audits of commercial firms. Currently there are about 300 members concerned with this type of work which involves 580 quoted firms with a total market capitalization of £2700 million. Qualification as a member of the IRE – which dates from 1953 – is obtained by completing a three-year training period and either graduating with a university degree in economics or business administration, or passing the Institute's own examinations. There is a minimum age requirement of 25 years. Although a réviseur d'enterprises may undertake work of an accounting nature, he must do this in a private capacity and not as part of his work as a statutory examiner. Any company selling shares to the public must appoint at least one statutory examiner (commissaire réviseur) and although such a person need not have Belgian nationality or residence, or have an accounting training, in the case of a public company (SA) at least one of the Commissaires must be a member of the IRE.

Most qualified accountants tend to be members of the Collège National des Experts Comptables although there are other organizations. The designation expert comptable does not, as yet, have any legal status. Membership of the Collège is obtained in a somewhat similar manner to that of the IRE, namely, by undergoing a five year training period with a member of the Collège followed by a professional examination in the applications of accounting. Preliminary examinations are required in accounting technique, law, administrative organization, economics, mathematics, statistics and ethics or, alternatively appropriate exemptions are granted to graduates in economics, financial or actuarial studies. A member must be at least 30 years old. It is possible for a person to qualify separately for membership of both bodies. There are currently about 1600 members of the Collège of whom something like one third are in public practice, the others being employed either in commerce, industry or accounting firms. The services offered by Experts Comptables include investigations, business and tax consultancy, liquidation, trustee and receivership work, and asset valuations.

Both professions, auditing and accounting, are governed by Codes of Ethics, that of the IRB being particularly restrictive. Members must practise in their own name. They cannot undertake any commercial activity, engage in directorships, partake in any form of salaried or contractual employment, or undertake work outside their own profession as auditors. The Code was promulgated in 1957 by the Minister of Economic Affairs and has the force of law. The Institut must authorize a réviseur's appointment as a commissaire réviseur and approve his fee. It also has the power to carry out disciplinary procedures. In the case of the Experts Comptables, a Code of Ethics was established by the College and contains pronouncements on such things as professional conduct and relationships. It stresses the necessity of a member's independence but does not ban a member having a financial interest in a client.

Statutory Requirements

Belgian legislation governing limited companies is contained in the Belgian Commercial Code, largely enacted before the turn of the century but incorporating also the 1935 Companies Act and amended in some respects by more recent Decrees. Although considerable attempts at company law reform have been initiated since the 1935 Act – one such attempt culminating in a draft Bill in 1947 – no comprehensive reform has yet been enacted. The statutory requirements of the Commercial Code therefore tend to be imprecise, the more detailed requirements being imposed by tax legislation. The main statutory requirements are included in the summary given later in this chapter.

Standards

Auditing

There are no recommended auditing standards although it is understood that the Collège is attempting to recommend certain auditing procedures. The methods that are in use are an amalgam of the requirements of the Commercial Code and those of the tax laws. The former requires the commissaires réviseurs to observe (and if necessary to call the attention of the shareholders to) the acts of management, as well as to report on the accounts. This report must verify the cash and securities held. The tax laws are largely instrumental in deciding the bases of valuation in operation, since the accounts for tax purposes must be identical with the filed accounts.

Reporting

There is no standard form of auditor's report. Usually, two reports are presented. There is a short statutory report by the commissaire which:

1   Certifies the cash and securities held.
2   States the agreement of the accounts with the books of account.
3   Recommends that the accounts as presented be approved.

A long report is presented to the directors, usually orientated to the 'minimum position', that is that the position is at least as satisfactory as the accounts disclose. Accordingly there can be no opinion expressed as to a 'true or fair view' of the state of the company's affairs. The directors are also required to submit a report to the shareholders detailing the names and addresses of any partly paid up shareholders and the amount unpaid, together with the distribution of profits.

Accounting

There are no recommendations on accounting principles, those standards that are in operation largely being induced by tax legislation and procedure. The fact that any expenses claimed must be charged in the financial accounts certainly influences a number of practices, and often induces what in the UK would be regarded as distortions of the income and valuation principles. A government advisory body is recommending the adoption of a national accounting plan on the lines of the French Plan Comptable in order to improve the disclosure of financial information. Current practice is set out in the summary.

Extra-statutory Requirements

The financial scene in Belgium, as in most of the Continental European countries, is dominated by private bank holding companies, state institutions and a preponderance of small, unquoted companies. There is, therefore, a narrow stock market, a lack of private interest in the provision of risk capital, and a reluctance on the part of managements to provide more than the statutory minimum of information. There has, therefore, been little pressure for the introduction of extra-statutory requirements.

Professional Bodies

No mandatory controls of an extra-statutory nature are exercised as yet by the professional bodies over their members. However, a number of recommendations have been published which include a standard chart of accounts, the form and content of financial statements, accounting principles, auditing standards and disclosure practices.

Stock Exchange

Although the role of the banks in Belgian investment is now quite marked, this is a comparatively recent development and was led by the National Savings Bank rather than the commercial banks. Indeed, the regulations governing bank investment activities were only relaxed in 1967 to allow permanent portfolio holdings covering issues by other companies. Although the main Stock Exchange (Brussels) is governed by a Council, the main regulatory body is the Commission Bancaire (CB). The function of this commission is to coordinate the approach of commercial companies to the capital market and to protect prospective investors against false information. The Commission dates from 1935 and has power to approve, recommend modification, postpone and/or publicize proposed share issues, takeover bids or requests for quotation on the part of companies. It also has extensive powers of supervision over deposit banks and investment funds.

Financial reporting requirements There are no formal requirements concerning the publication of financial accounts by industrial companies other than that they be examined by a commissaire reviseur. Although the CB has attempted to improve reporting standards it has not been successful as yet since it has no control over annual statements produced by industrial companies.

Listing requirements and prospectuses It is in the area of information required in a prospectus offering shares to the public that the CB has substantially improved practice. In this area, statutory requirements, as outlined in the Commercial Code, cover details of objects, capital structure, unpaid capital, assets to be purchased out of proceeds, and directors. In addition the CB requires a schedule of liabilities and contingent liabilities, the purpose of the issue, details of underwriting arrangements and particulars of shares held by interested parties. It can investigate the adequacy and accuracy of the information presented to it, although there is no requirement for an independent accountant's report. In addition to the formal approval of the CB to a listing application, the Stock Exchange requires a minimum capital, and the publication of the balance sheet of the firm over the previous two years.

Takeover and Merger Requirements

There is no established Code covering takeover and merger practices other than the approval procedure adopted by the CB, since 1964, in the case of a public offer for the purchase of shares or bonds. In addition, there has been a move by the professional bodies to promote the use of generally accepted accounting principles and concepts of fairness, in the preparation of reports concerning mergers and acquisitions. A number of 'Recommendations Relating to Information Published by Companies' were published in 1968 as a result of a study undertaken by representatives of banking, accounting, and financial interests. These Recommendations are not mandatory.

Summary of the Principal Areas of Current Accounting and Reporting Requirements in Belgium

Accountant's Report to be Included in a Prospectus for the Sale of Securities

There is no requirement for an independent accountant's report or for a profit forecast. However, considerable detail as to the purpose of the issue, details of underwriting arrangements and particulars of shares held by interested parties are required by the Banking Commission. In addition, the Commission requires a schedule of liabilities and contingent liabilities, and can investigate the accuracy of the information presented to it. The Stock Exchange requires the previous two years' balance sheets to be published and the Commercial Code requires details of the Company's objects, capital structure, unpaid capital, directors, and assets to be purchased out of the proceeds of the issue.

Form and Content of Published Accounts

All limited companies are required to file an audited copy of the financial accounts at the local commercial court. These accounts must be audited and consist of the balance sheet and profit and loss account, profit appropriation statement, an analysis of share capital, together with details of any holders of unpaid capital and a list of directors and auditors. There is no requirement to file a copy of the auditor's report. The profit appropriation must be in accordance with the shareholders' authorization. The financial accounts must also be published in the official gazette, and copies must be sent to trade unions and the taxing authorities.

There is no fixed format for a balance sheet (other than for banks and certain insurance companies) but there must be shown separately: fixed assets, current assets, capital, reserves and surplus, secured and unsecured debentures and other liabilities. A legal reserve must be maintained but no valuation principles are outlined.

There are no requirements concerning the profit and loss account other than that 'appropriate' depreciation shall be charged. Consequently, the profit and loss account is normally presented in an abridged form.

There are no requirements for the presentation of consolidated accounts and such accounts are specifically precluded from being substituted for the balance sheets of individual companies. Consequently, the presentation of consolidated statements is hardly ever practised. Investments in subsidiaries are shown at cost, less any (undisclosed) contingency reserves. Accounting for subsidiaries on an equity basis is rarely practised.

There is no standard form of auditor's report. Usually two reports are presented:

1 A short form certificate as to the compliance with the law and the verification of cash and securities.
2 A long form report, including the certificate, which is made to the management and would require them to bring any irregular acts of management to the attention of the shareholders. This report also explains and supplements certain of the balances in the financial accounts.

The directors must report to the shareholders and the supervisory board, if one is in existence. Such a report would include a statement showing the proposed profit allocation and details of any partly paid up share capital, including the names and addresses of such partly paid up shareholders.

Current Practice

Fixed assets Normally valued at cost, although in certain cases assets held in 1946 were revalued, such revaluation being credited to a special reserve account which was not available for distribution. Costs associated with a fixed asset may also be initially capitalized and depreciated at a rate different from that applying to the relevant asset.

Depreciation is normally charged in accordance with tax rates, on a straight-line basis, and must be included in the financial accounts at the amount required to qualify for tax relief. Accelerated depreciation in accordance with tax rules is charged and, in poor years, the charge for depreciation is likely to be deferred until such time as maximum tax benefit can be obtained. Such inconsistencies would not be disclosed nor considered worthy of comment by the statutory auditor. Where assets have been revalued, depreciation is only allowable – and therefore charged – on the basis of original cost. Figures are shown at cost or reappraised values, accumulated depreciation either being deducted therefrom or shown as a reserve on the liabilities side of the balance sheet.

Goodwill and intangibles These are generally shown at cost, but are written off either over the life of a relevant asset or over a short period. Goodwill may be allowed, as it is amortized, for tax purposes according to specific rules.

Investments There is seldom any differentiation made between investments in affiliates, subsidiaries or others and they are valued according to cost or market rules. It is unlikely that market values are disclosed, even in the case of quoted investments. However, a list of investments is usually given.

Current assets and stocks These are valued on the cost or market basis, but with provisions against debtors only recognized for tax purposes when the debt becomes irrecoverable. In practice stocks are likely to be valued for tax purposes, on an individual item basis, cost to include overheads, and by an average, specific or FIFO method. LIFO and base stock methods are not permitted for tax purposes and therefore not used in financial accounts. It is unlikely that the basis of stock pricing would be disclosed. The tax rules permit certain commodity stocks to be reduced to the lowest prices ruling on world markets within the last five years and it is not uncommon for stocks generally to be written down in order to smooth income between periods. No disclosure of such practices is likely. Distinction is made between immovable and realizable assets.

Deferred charges Preliminary expenses are amortized over a relatively short period and, if in accordance with tax rules, such amortization will be allowed.

Liabilities Differentiation tends to be between long- and short-term although secured liabilities would also be distinguished. There is little disclosure of interest rates or duration other than the one-year dividing line implied between long- and short-term.

Reserves and provisions A legal reserve is required to be maintained of at least 10% of the share capital and, until it reaches this proportion, 5% of profits must be appropriated annually. Such reserve may only be used to absorb losses, or, if in excess of 10%, may be capitalized. Restricted reserves are nondistributable and are often stipulated as such by the company's articles. Free reserves are the appropriations of profits authorized by the shareholders for distribution. Any premiums on shares may be added to such free reserves, or capitalized according to the shareholders' wishes. Any surplus remaining from the revaluation of property or other fixed assets would appear in a specific reserve. Secret reserves are common, arising from excessive depreciation, stock and investment write-downs and over-provision for contingencies. Reserves are not always shown within the 'equity' section of the balance sheet, even if 'free'. It is not normal practice to show movements on reserves.

Share capital Shares need not have a par value. They may be in the form of bearer shares, but they cannot be repurchased by the company. Share capital must be fully subscribed and, in the case of bearer shares, fully paid up before issue. In the case of registered shares, issue may be made when 20% of the price is paid, unless the price is in kind, in which case the share must be fully paid up on issue. Shareholders' equity is not necessarily shown because of the possible classing of depreciation as a reserve and the separate placing of profit available for distribution. Bonus issues are generally made at par and dividends are part of the distributed profit figure shown on the balance sheet, proposed dividends not normally being provided.

Accounting for acquisitions and mergers There is little standardization of practice other than the lack of use of the pooling of interests method.

Income statement There are no legal classification requirements for the profit and loss account which, accordingly, is normally presented in a very abridged form. Neither sales nor cost of sales is normally disclosed and the account normally commences with gross profit. Depreciation for the year is usually shown as a separate item and, because of the tax requirements for items claimed to be charged in the financial accounts, is orientated towards taxation rather than finance. The basis of the provision is unlikely to be disclosed. Wages and salaries are unlikely to be shown, although financial and debt charges and investment and financial income are likely to be shown in the aggregate. Prior-year or extraordinary items are seldom distinguished.

Taxation accounting is normal practice but there is no deferred system of accounting for differences between estimates and actual liabilities. In any case, most tax liabilities are paid within the period in which the income is earned because of penalties for late payment.

Appropriations are not normally included in the statement although an analysis of the allocation and approved distributions are normally published. Payments to directors for fees, salaries, etc, are normally regarded as appropriations.

Other points As mentioned earlier, the financial statements may only serve to show the 'minimum position' and as such the overriding concepts are those of conservatism and the tax rules. Supplementary notes are unusual although memorandum accounts with regard to contingencies are sometimes given. Changes in accounting methods, post-date events or capital commitments are unlikely to be disclosed and comparative figures are only required for quoted companies.

Current Trends

The main trend is an increasing interest in improving standards of accounting, auditing and disclosure. In this connection, the practice of issuing Recommendations recently followed by the professional bodies has already been referred to in the previous section. Perhaps the most significant indication of the move to improve standards is the expressed Government intention of adopting a mandatory chart of accounts, a Plan Comptable, modelled on the French pattern, in order to impose at least minimum standards of presentation and disclosure.

The developing accounting system in Belgium, with its dependence on the taxation legislation, implies a macroeconomic orientation within the context of Mueller's identified patterns described in Chapter 1. The emergence of proposals for a uniform chart and plan of accounts modelled on the French system is likely to increase this orientation.

6

Denmark

Type of Business Unit

Companies with Limited Liability

These companies are governed by the Companies Act of 1930, substantially amended by a new Companies Act 1973. The 1973 legislation, largely finalized in 1964, forms a 'Nordic' companies law, harmonizing much of the legislation relating to limited companies throughout Denmark, Finland, Norway and Sweden. The legislation also anticipates many of the current proposals for company law harmonization within the EEC. Companies with limited liability may be:

1 Public companies (Aktieselskab – A/S). Prior to 1974 this type of organization was basically the only form of limited company allowed under Danish law. An A/S must have at least three founder members, all of whom (or a majority if more than three) must be both Danish nationals and residents of at least five years' standing. Shares are freely transferable, and must be fully paid up within one year of issue. There is a minimum share capital requirement of DKr 100000 (£7000) – prior to 1 January 1974, DKr 10000 (£700) – and existing A/S firms are allowed until the end of 1976 to achieve the new minimum figure. If the share capital is DKr 400000 (£28000) or more, or where the number of employees exceeds 50, there must be at least three directors. In any case where employees exceed 50 there must be, in addition to the three directors, a further two employee-elected representatives on the board. There may be a supervisory board elected by shareholders, in which case there must be at least five members, some of whom may be employees but not directors or managers. There are

national and residential qualifications connected with the posts of director and executive manager. Annual audited accounts must be filed and made available for inspection. A request may be made – and is usually granted – for non-publication. Quoted companies must have at least two auditors, and at least one must be a state authorized public accountant (SR). Unquoted companies must have at least one SR auditor or, where total assets are less than DKr 2 million (£140000) at least one SR or one registered accountant (RR)

2 Private companies (Anpartsselskab – APS) authorized by a new law which came into effect on 1 January 1974. An APS need only have one member but shares may be transferable. Share capital must be at least DKr 30000 (£2100). The regulations concerning directors and employee representatives, where share capital is DKr 400000 and/or employees exceed 50, are similar to those for the A/S. Where total assets exceed DKr 2 million, or where the APS is one of a group of companies where any one company's assets exceed that figure or total group assets exceed DKr 10 million, annual audited accounts – including consolidated statements – must be filed. In other cases, only an abridged Balance Sheet must be filed. Where total assets exceed DKr 2 million, at least one of the auditors must be an SR; below that figure there are no stipulations as to the qualification of the statutory auditor.

Cooperatives

Cooperatives are an important form of agricultural organization, although outside the scope of company legislation. They may be:

1 Andelsselskab (AMBA) – with limited liability.
2 Forbrugs-og Produktions-Foreninger with unlimited liability.

Partnerships

Partnerships may be:

1 General (Interessentskab – I/S) following the normal pattern of joint and several liability.
2 Limited (Kommanditselskab – K/S), an association with at least one unlimited general partner, which may be a limited company, and one or more partners whose liability is limited to their capital contribution.
3 Limited partnership company (Kommandit-Aktieselskab – K/A), an association similar to the K/S but having the limited members' contribution evidenced by shares. Although rare, this form of organization is now legislated for by the new Companies Act.

Sole Traders with Unlimited Liability

Branches of Foreign Corporations

A branch of a foreign corporation may be set up provided that reciprocal rights of establishment exist in the other country. Normally, the national and residential requirements applicable to directors and managers of domestic companies apply to the manager of the branch, who must also possess power of attorney in order that the branch activities can be made to comply with Danish law.

Business Records

Companies are required to keep minute books, annual accounts and auditor's reports and work programme, together with a share register and register of directors' and managers' share dealings. Unlike many European systems, the Danish system specifically authorizes, in the 1959 Bookkeeping Act, the use of loose-leaf records for bookkeeping purposes subject to adequate control over their use.

The Accounting Profession

The accounting profession in Denmark is generally organized within the Foreningen af Statsautoriserede Revisorer (FSR) the Institute of State-authorized Public Accountants. The FSR was founded in 1912 but its official recognition dates mainly from the 1930–1933 laws concerning companies and state authorization of public accountants. A licence to practise as a state-authorized public accountant is granted by the Ministry of Trade, Industry and Shipping and is dependent upon an applicant being qualified by examination, experience and certain other requirements. The examinations are conducted by a board on which the Ministry of Commerce, the universities, the Tax Department, industry and the profession are represented. They consist of written and oral tests in economics, trade law, taxation, auditing and accounting theory and practice. Where a student has obtained a diploma in accounting from a school of economics and business administration he can be exempted from all but the auditing and accounting practice examinations. An alternative method is to complete a five-year full-time course culminating in the Master of Commerce degree in auditing; this carries exemption from all but the final professional examination. In addition, a candidate for a practising licence must have had at least three years' experience in the office of a state-authorized public accountant, he must be at least 25 years old, a Danish subject and resident in Denmark. He must not have been declared incapable of managing his own affairs or controlling his estate, and must sign a solemn declaration as to his intention of performing his function diligently, faithfully and conscientiously. Although the minimum age limit is 25 years, in practice the average age of such applicants is between 30 and 35.

The duties and liabilities of a state-authorized public accountant were first legalized in 1933. The Act allowed the formation of limited companies of practitioners, provided a majority of the directors and managers are licensed. It prohibits the participation of practitioners in:

1 Trade or industry generally.
2 Mixed practices of non-state-authorized accountants or attorneys.
3 Any employment other than in an auditing and accounting business.

In addition, a licensee is restricted as to the number of inexperienced assistants he can employ. A state-authorized public accountant, as well as auditing and reporting on financial statements, undertakes:

1 Business and tax consultancy.
2 Investigatory work, particularly on behalf of creditors, pricing agencies and potential borrowers.
3 Systems installation.

Membership of the FSR, currently approximately 1000, is restricted to state-authorized public accountants and may be retained by members who have ceased to practise provided that there is no conflict of interest. There is a Code of Ethics which forms part of the Institute's bye-laws, and which governs: the relationships of members between themselves and with clients; members' acceptance of work; and fees and commissions. The Code also restricts advertising. The Institute has disciplinary powers where its rules are infringed, and in addition a 1968 law contains certain provisions regarding the rights, duties and responsibilities of auditors.

A law passed in 1970 instituted the qualification of Registrerede Revisorer whose professional body is the Association of Registered Accountants (Foreningen af Registrerede Revisorer). The law was introduced as a means of increasing the number of qualified accountants (although at a junior level to the SR) and to cater for the needs of small and medium sized businesses. In order to become registered with the Ministry of Commerce, a candidate must:

1 Follow a basic 140-hour part-time course in bookkeeping and the preparation of financial statements.
2 Complete a three-year, 390-hour course in accountancy and auditing.
3 Be engaged on relevant work with an audit firm.

Although the requirements may be completed within five years, there is a minimum age requirement of 25 years. The restrictions placed on the RR are much less severe than those on the SR and thus he is likely to be engaged on accountancy work within firms and may also be a board member. Currently, there are approximately 1000 Registered Accountants, of whom the large majority are members of the Association.

Although in practice most auditors are state-authorized, the Companies Act does not stipulate that they must be so. A qualified auditor, according to the Act, is anyone who is of age, of good repute, and not divested of the management of his estate. He must not, however, be in the employ of the audited company or its employees – in any capacity – nor can he be related to such employees. Except in the case of banks, certain insurance companies and pension funds (and within the stipulations regarding limited companies), a person may be appointed as auditor if he possesses 'the insight and experience in accounting and financial matters required for the execution of his duties, having regard to the type and scope of the company's activities.'

Although there are only some 200 or so quoted companies in Denmark, there are upwards of 25 000 A/S companies registered. It is likely that many of these companies will transfer to the more appropriate APS form, now that this is available, and mirror the German experience with the GMBH form of organization.

Statutory Requirements

Danish companies are largely regulated by the Companies Act of 1930, since amended, and by the Bookkeeping Law of 1959. The legal requirements tend to be vague and superficial, most of the detailed requirements concerning disclosure and valuation principles emanating from the tax legislation. However, Denmark has now passed the 1973 Companies legislation differentiating the large from the small limited company. This legislation, governing the larger company and anticipating forthcoming EEC company law harmonization, is concerned with publicity, voting rights and structure. The new legislation places much more emphasis on disclosure of information, including the extent of taxation distortions, in the case of the large or quoted limited company. The main requirements are set out in the summary.

Standards

Auditing

There are no recommended auditing standards although the FSR has introduced some recommendations as to specific practice areas as a result of opinions published in answer to queries. Legislation governing the profession states only that the auditor shall carry out his audit according to accepted professional practice. An auditor must be allowed to carry out a sufficient investigation to enable him to give an opinion as to the accuracy of facts presented, although his verification will tend to be restricted to cash, bank amounts and securities held.

Reporting

There is no standard form of auditor's report, the usual form being very brief, stating only that the audited accounts have been examined and they are in accordance with the books of account. However, an auditing register is maintained by companies which details:

1 The work carried out by the auditor.
2 Whether he has been able satisfactorily to fulfil all his obligations and received all the information he requires.
3 Whether the accounts have been prepared in conformity with the company law, the company's own bye-laws and, where applicable, the tax laws.

The register will also contain any comments considered necessary by the auditor as to the results generally and the procedures specifically carried out by the company's management. The auditing register is not available to shareholders. Since 1 January 1974 the auditors must bring to the attention of shareholders any point deemed to be important for an evaluation of the company's financial position or other matters of interest.

Accounting

There are no recommendations on accounting principles. Current practice is very much influenced by the model set of financial statements published by the FSR in 1970 as a recommendation on the form and content of accounts. Much of this is included in the new company laws which set out certain provisions for the presentation of accounts in the balance sheet and profit and loss account. Current practice is outlined in detail in the summary below.

Extra-statutory Requirements

Share issues are a negligible source of capital for Danish industry, the most important sources being savings, depreciation write-offs and foreign commercial credits. Thus the Copenhagen Stock Exchange is much more of a bond market than a share market. With so little recourse to external sources of finance there has been little need for extra-statutory requirements.

Professional Bodies

As yet the FSR has not issued any mandatory statements as to standards of accounting, auditing and reporting, although it has published replies to specific problems raised by members in the form of recommendations as to preferred practices, model financial statements and disclosure of information.

Stock Exchange

For the reasons outlined at the beginning of this section the stock market in Denmark is small and shareholders are few in number. Applications for listing and dealings are reviewed by a Stock Exchange Board.

Financial reporting requirements There are no Stock Exchange controls concerning financial statements other than the requirement that such statements must be audited by two auditors, one of whom must be a state-authorized public accountant.

Listing requirements and prospectuses The Stock Exchange Board reviews all applications and requires a prospectus containing general information about the company, the purpose of the issue, details of the face value, issue price and method of payment of the shares to be issued, and the treatment of any over-subscription. Audited financial statements for at least one year must be filed with the prospectus and, whilst these are not required to be published with the prospectuses, they are available for prospective purchasers. Companies applying for a listing must fulfil minimum capital requirements.

Takeover and Merger Requirements

There is no code of permissible practice concerning takeovers and mergers other than the overall review procedure administered by the Stock Exchange Board.

Summary of the Principal Areas of Current Accounting and Reporting Requirements in Denmark

Accountant's Report to be Included in a Prospectus for the Sale of Securities

There is no requirement for an independent accountant's report, nor for a profits fore-cast. The Stock Exchange Board requires a prospectus which must detail the issue details and procedures, and must be accompanied by audited financial statements covering at least the last year. Although the financial statements are available to prospective pur-chasers, they are not required to be generally published with the prospectus.

Form and Content of Published Accounts

All companies must file a copy of the audited annual accounts, consisting of a balance sheet, profit and loss account, notes and annual report with the Registrar of Companies. However, companies may request that such reports should be classed as confidential and it has been estimated that 60% of Danish companies have, in the past, availed themselves of this concession. The new APS form avoids this situation. There is no prescribed form of balance sheet but the following items must be separately shown:

1 Intangible assets, ships, aircraft and real estate.
2 Short- and long-term liabilities.
3 Contingent liabilities.
4 The amounts of mortgages, uncovered securities and guarantees.
5 The legal reserve.

There are few legal requirements relating to the profit and loss account. The statement must give a satisfactory explanation of the net result of operations, and sales and certain other income and expenses must be separately shown. Since the new laws became effec-tive on 1 January 1974, consolidated statements must be prepared and filed. Investments in subsidiaries are usually shown at cost, and accounting on an equity basis is not normally practised.

The auditor's report is normally very brief and restricted to a certification of his examination of the accounts and books of accounts and that the accounts have been prepared in compliance with the law and company bye-laws. However, the auditor must prepare an audit minute, or register, which:

1 Details the work carried out by the auditor.
2 States the extent of his satisfaction with the information provided for him.
3 Indicates whether he has been able to fulfil his legal obligations.
4 Includes the certification as to conformity with the law and company bye-laws.
5 Comments on the results shown by the accounts where the auditor deems it necessary to do so.
6 Similarly comments on any specific management procedures adopted.

There is no standard form for either the certificate or the minute. The certificate –

together with 5 above and other matters of interest – is included with the accounts for filing and publication, but the audit minute is restricted to the company and not made available to shareholders.

A directors' report – a 'report on the administration' – has to be signed by all the directors and filed with the annual accounts. Such a report must amplify the financial statements where necessary in order to allow a meaningful interpretation. The report should also disclose any significant events relating to the company, the remuneration of management, and the proposed profit distribution.

Current Practice

Fixed assets Undervaluation of fixed assets is permitted by current Danish law as it only stipulates maximum values. The value in this case is cost, unless the excess on a re-valuation of a fixed asset has been used to write down other fixed assets, to cover operating losses, or placed to a special reserve for such purposes. The allowable items under the tax rules need not be 'booked'. Depreciation must be charged on any fixed asset in order to reflect decrease in value due to usage. It must be charged irrespective of the existence of profit or loss but cannot exceed an amount calculated on original cost of the asset. Fixed assets are often shown net of accumulated depreciation.

Goodwill and intangibles Purchased goodwill may be shown at cost but must be written off within ten years. Other intangibles must be written off within five years.

Investments These must be valued at a figure not exceeding cost or market price, excepting that quoted securities must not be valued at a figure exceeding the quoted buying rate at the date of the year-end. Details of market value in other than quoted securities would not be disclosed.

Current assets and stocks Values must not exceed the lower of cost or market price. Stocks are normally considerably undervalued in that the tax regulations allow a deduction of up to 30% of the cost or market figure although it does not have to be 'booked'. The inclusion of overheads in cost is optional, and average or FIFO methods are customarily used. There is normally no disclosure of the extent of the undervaluation of stock, even though this might fluctuate from year to year, but there must be disclosure of the method of valuation used.

Deferred charges Formation expenses generally, including capital issue expenses and discounts on debentures, must be written off to profit and loss account in the year in which they are incurred.

Liabilities Long-term liabilities must be shown separately from short-term liabilities, although the latter are not normally subtotalled. Details of secured liabilities are shown but it is not usual to disclose terms or duration of long-term debts.

Reserves and provisions A legal (statutory) reserve of at least 10% of share capital must be built up by annual appropriations of 10% of profits after depreciation and accumulated losses from earlier years have been covered. Once the reserve reaches 10% of share capital, 5% of the profits is appropriated annually. Any share premiums must be added to this reserve if it is below one quarter of the share capital. The reserve can only be used to absorb losses and then only to the extent that they cannot be covered by the year's surplus or other, nonstatutory, reserves. Until the statutory reserve attains 10% of the share capital, shareholders are restricted to a dividend of 6% per annum. Other, free reserves, are also normally maintained, including reserves for future investments. Secret reserves, once commonplace, arising from excessive depreciation, stock and investment write downs and over-provision for contingencies, are much less likely under the new legislation. Movements on reserves must now be disclosed.

Share capital Shares must have a par value but, under the new legislation, cannot be repurchased by the company except in exceptional circumstances. Any such shares held by a company, and not disposed of within two years, must be given a nil value in the balance sheet. At least 10% of the share capital must be paid up on registration, the remainder within one year. Premiums on shares must be put to the legal reserve where it does not exceed one quarter of the share capital otherwise they can be dealt with at the shareholders' discretion. Shareholders' equity is not necessarily shown as one figure on the balance sheet. Bonus issues are made at par and dividends (proposed) are normally shown in an appropriations section of the income statement.

Accounting for acquisitions and mergers There is little standard practice and pooling of interests method is not recognized.

Income statement There are no legal classification requirements and therefore the account tends to be in short form usually commencing with gross profit. Turnover must be disclosed except where it is detrimental to the company. Wages and salaries are not normally shown. Depreciation is normally shown in the aggregate but, although the basis of calculation is not normally disclosed, any change in policy must be described in the notes. Charges and income details tend to be shown in aggregate amounts. Extraordinary items or prior-year adjustments should be specifically referred to. Profits or losses on sale of fixed assets should be shown separately. The taxation charge due on the current year's income must be shown separately from any taxation adjustments as a result of changes in earlier years' assessments. Details of any deferred taxation liability must be given in the notes if not shown separately in the accounts. Appropriations are normally shown in a separate appropriation section of the profit and loss account.

Other Points The financial accounts, together with the obligatory notes, are now made much more informative and meaningful as a result of the 1973 Companies Act, despite a continued conservative orientation exemplified by the maximum valuation rules for assets. The legislation specifically requires a note to be made of any significant changes in accounting policies or of other material information, which would include capital commitments and post-date events. Comparative figures are normally shown.

Current Trends

Current activity tends to be concentrated on two fronts:

1   There is a general move to improve the standards of accounting, auditing and disclosure of information.
2   There are distinct proposals concerning an increase in the extent of employee shareholding in industry.

Statutory Trends

The 1973 company laws attempting to harmonize legislation between Denmark, Finland, Norway and Sweden, have done a great deal to improve the quality of information provided by the quoted and larger limited companies. Although being instituted in a somewhat piecemeal manner, they provide a much needed boost to attempts by the Danish accounting profession to improve standards generally. One of the most significant effects is the movement away from taxation accounting, allowing separate profit computations for tax purposes from the profits shown in the financial statements.

Attempts are being made to encourage shareholding by workers. It has been suggested that employers should set up funds to be invested in equity shares in the names of their workers, and which may be cashed by the workers after five years. The proposals provide that workers' shareholdings shall not exceed 50% of the total equity. Initial opposition to these proposals has been strong, and the implementation of the necessary legislation has been delayed until some future parliamentary session.

Professional Trends

Following the issue of a model set of financial statements in 1970, the FSR has started to issue exposure drafts recommending practices concerning financial statements. Thus recommendations have been made regarding the disclosure of the basis of asset valuations and movements of fixed assets, and it is suggested that a standard form of audit report should be adopted which would require the auditor to state an opinion as to the 'truth' and 'fairness' of the accounts.

The Danish accounting system remains orientated towards taxation accounting, excepting in the case of the larger companies, and even under the new laws is very heavily creditor-biased. It may still, therefore, be described as falling within the macroeconomic pattern as defined by Mueller and described in Chapter 1.

7

France

Type of Business Unit

Companies with Limited Liability

Such companies are controlled by the Companies Act of 1966 and the French Commercial Code generally. Business units with limited liability are comprised of:

1   Public companies (Société Anonyme – SA) which must have at least seven founder members and a definite life-span (not exceeding 99 years) stated in the articles of association. Share capital must be at least Fr 500 000 (approximately £45 000) in the case of an SA with unlimited right of share transfer, or Fr 100 000 (£9000) where the company does not invite the public to subscribe for any of its shares or bonds. An SA cannot normally purchase its own shares. Although the traditional structure of a president and board of directors is still retained, the system of having an independent supervisory board as well as a board of directors (as operates in Germany) is now permitted as an alternative structure. Annual audited accounts must be filed and, in the case of quoted companies with total assets in excess of Fr 10 million (£900 000) they must be published, together with the audited directors' report.
2   Private companies (Société à Responsibilité Limitée – SARL) which have a minimum subscribed share capital of Fr 20 000 (£1800), a defined life, restricted rights of share transfer, and a minimum of two and a maximum of 50 members. Any SARL with a share capital exceeding Fr 300 000 (£27 000) must have its accounts audited and all SARLs must file a copy of financial statements. A SARL does not issue share certificates.

Cooperatives

Cooperatives are not normally found in France, but there are two specific forms of organization for the private consortium or pooling arrangement. These are Société en Participation, which is basically a joint venture with no separate legal entity; and Groupement d'intérêt Économique which is part joint venture and part private company. On registration it has a separate legal entity, and members are normally jointly and severally liable for debts (unless the creditors have agreed to a contract limiting liability). It is not regarded as a commercial entity because it need not have the making of profit as an objective.

Partnerships

Partnerships may be:

1   General (Societé en Nom Collectif), which is the normal commercial form, with a separate legal entity in French law, even though partners are taxed individually. Where partners' names do not appear in the firm name it must be styled '. . . et compagnie' (et CIE).
2   Limited (Société en Commandite Simple), with at least one general partner.
3   Limited with shares (Société en Commandite Par Actions), where shareholders have transferable shares and limited liability but also with at least one general partner.
4   Civil (Société Civile Professionelle), formed for firms of professionals, particularly auditors, in place of the previously permitted companies of auditors.

Sole Traders with Unlimited Liability

Branches of Foreign Enterprises

A branch of a foreign enterprise is not recognized under French law as a separate legal entity and its liabilities are those of its parent company. A subsidiary may be organized as a French corporation, having a separate legal identity and being subject to the same legal and tax treatment as a domestic French company.

Business Records

The basic records required by the Commercial Code are the general journal and a balances book, while the Code of Labour requires a payroll journal. All of these should be bound, prenumbered and stamped by a judge or mayor. In addition, a share register is normally kept, and the Plan Comptable (Accounting Plan) requires the keeping of a general ledger and subsidiary books as necessary for a particular firm. The Plan Comptable, brought into being in 1947 and subsequently revised, and which currently has about 40 divisions for the different industry sectors, is a standard accounting system which prescribes a chart of accounts for national use. It has been obligatory for all enterprises as from 1970.

The Accounting Profession

The position of the accounting profession in France is notable because of the separation of the auditing and accounting activities, decreed by law in 1966. The auditing profession is organized under the Ministry of Justice whereas the accounting profession comes under the auspices of the Ministry of Economics and Finance.

The pre-eminent body within the accounting profession is L'Ordre des Experts Comptables et des Comptables Agrées, established in 1942 and subsequently amalgamated with a number of different accounting bodies. As a result of legislation passed in 1968 L'Ordre will combine with L'Institut Francais des Experts Comptables (the other accounting body of any repute) to form a unified accounting profession. Part of the unification procedure is that the 'Comptables Agrées' part of L'Ordre – who would be regarded in the UK as sub-professional bookkeepers – should cease to be eligible for recruitment to L'Ordre from 1968. There are transitional arrangements to 1975 for Comptables Agrées with ten years' professional experience. A number of Experts Comptables are also separately qualified and authorized to undertake statutory audits. Membership of L'Ordre does not carry any right to perform audits, and is restricted to qualified accountants actually in practice *and* working as principals. This restriction excludes them from salaried employment other than as employees of registered companies of Experts Comptables. Prior to 1966 members were permitted to practise within a limited company structure provided that three of the major shareholders were themselves members of L'Ordre. Although this structure is still allowed, any such companies formed since 1966 cannot undertake statutory audits even where the members of the company are individually qualified and authorized to do so. Apart from the company structure, Experts Comptables also practise in partnership form and as sole practitioners, the latter form being traditionally the more common. Until 1970 an Expert Comptable was precluded from employing more than five salaried accountants – other than articled students – but in 1970 this number was increased to ten. This statutorily-induced tendency to small accounting firms has retarded the development of the accounting profession in France.

Current membership of the accounting profession, ie L'Ordre and L'Institut, is approximately 11 000. In order to qualify as a member of L'Ordre a person must pass a three-stage examination covering papers in mercantile, company and industrial law, economics, financial and management accounting, auditing, and one of the following: advanced law and tax law, business organization and management, or European and international economic relations. Exemption from some of the foregoing papers is granted to 'relevant' graduates. In addition to the written papers, a student must have undergone a three-year articleship, with at least one of those years in the office of an Expert Comptable, and must also have submitted a thesis on an approved accounting topic. The minimum age for admittance to L'Ordre is 25 years although, in practice, most applicants are about 30 years of age.

The auditing function in France originated in 1867 in the Companies Charter which provided that all SAs must have their accounts examined by one or more Commissaires aux Comptes (Statutory Examiners). Such a person was appointed on behalf of the shareholders to keep a watch over the management board's activities (including the reporting of any illegal act on the board's part). The Commissaire was not required to certify the accounts nor to carry out an audit even though he might in the course of his duties have to enquire into certain transactions. Traditionally, the Commissaires were not necessarily accountants, but also came from the Civil Service or were administrators or engineers. The main criterion for their appointment was their independence from the particular board of directors and they could therefore be in other salaried employment; what they could not do was to be concerned, in any way, with the preparation of the accounts on which they were reporting. However, larger firms obviously needed the more conventional and complete kind of audit, and accordingly the Expert Comptable came to be employed – more as an agent of management – to carry out this function as an activity separate from that undertaken by the Commissaire aux Compte. A law passed in 1935 established rolls of approved Commissaires and also conditions of competency involving a qualifying examination in bookkeeping, accounting, mercantile and company law and taxation. The standard required by the examination is less stringent than that required of an Expert Comptable. However, in 1966, the Companies Act extended the statutory audit requirement to large SARLs, created the profession of Commissaires, fixed minimum fees, and – most importantly – laid upon the Commissaire the duty of certifying the truth and fairness of the accounts, assets and liabilities, and forming an opinion on certain management activities. In 1969 the requirements of the 1966 Act as to conditions of competency were extended to include a professional probationary period as well as an examination. It is significant that although an Expert Comptable can be registered as a Commissaire aux Compte the reverse is not true. Although the legislation fixed a scale of fees for statutory audits, these fees, based on company characteristics, are currently deemed to be inadequate for anything other than a most superficial investigation. Commissaires aux Comptes, who must be members of La Compagnie Nationale des Commissaires aux Comptes, currently number 6000, and their work covers upwards of 87000 SA companies, of which 830 are quoted with a total market capitalization of £9400 million. They also audit the larger SARLs. Commissaires are permitted to employ assistants and, since 1966, have been authorized to set up civil partnerships which replaced the limited companies previously permitted.

There is a rigid code of ethics which has been adopted by L'Ordre for its members. The code deals with the Expert Comptable's relationship with other members, clients, government officers and articled clerks. Members have to take an oath on admission regarding the exercise of their professional duty. In the case of Commissaires aux Compte the law prohibits a number of relationships, both as regards persons and property. In both cases great stress is laid upon independence, which is regarded, as in Germany, as a state of mind.

The profession in France is clearly divided into accounting and auditing functions. The accounting profession (L'Ordre) has a more rigorous entry requirement and a higher standing than applies to auditors, but its development has been retarded by the smallness of accounting firms. Both accounting and auditing professions have rigorous codes of ethics.

Statutory Requirements

The French Companies Act of 1966 is broadly equivalent, in aim if not in execution, to the UK Acts of 1948 and 1967, and supplements the French Commercial Code, itself updated in 1953. In addition, these legal requirements are buttressed by the Plan Comptable Generale which prescribes detailed accounting procedures, obligatory for all enterprises. The Plan contains a detailed chart of accounts, specifying classification, valuation and costing procedures, and prescribes the content and form of financial statements and final accounts. Its stated objectives are to:

Promote more reliable national economic and fiscal policies.
Assist in eliminating fiscal inequalities.
Minimize social misunderstandings by informing the public of the true distribution of national wealth.
Provide data for the study of market trends.
Improve healthy competition.
Aid in the development of fairer taxation.
Provide shareholders, suppliers and bankers with an opportunity to exercise their judgement more satisfactorily.
Aid governmental authorities in exercising controls.
Provide a clear and prompt view of financial results.
Permit analysis and comparison of manufacturing costs.

However, the apparent uniformity of accounting practice prescribed by the Plan Comptable is not matched either by the rules as to company registration or the interpretation of the Commercial Code. In the first case, the company's particulars are registered both nationally and locally, the latter register being determined by the jurisdiction of a particular court district, and the registrar being a clerk who takes no responsibility for the correctness or validity of the information recorded. In the second case, the legal code is interpreted by a notary within the court district, to a court composed entirely of unpaid lay judges drawn from the local business community. Thus there is no guarantee of uniformity from one district to another. The current statutory requirements relating to limited companies are summarized within the overall requirements set out in the summary.

Standards

Auditing

Professional auditing standards are only currently being evolved in France. From the foregoing description of the differences between the accounting and auditing professions this is hardly surprising. However, L'Ordre des Expert Comptables, together with the government and, latterly, La Compagnie Nationale des Commissaires aux Comptes have begun to issue tentative drafts for discussion in an attempt to formulate auditing standards. The auditor's report is largely a statement of fact, certifying the correctness of the balances, the financial statements and the accuracy of the directors' report insofar as it concerns the financial statements. Although the 1966 Companies Act provides that the auditor must certify the fairness, regularity, and consistency of the company's financial statements, there is little actual judgement involved in the task. The classification of accounts, form of financial statement and valuation procedures are all governed by the

Plan Comptable, supplemented by the tax laws.

Reporting

There is no standard form of auditor's report prescribed by law in France; there is considerable detail as to what he has to report on, but no guidance as to how he shall discharge his duties. Two reports are required:

1   A general report, usually in long form, which must:
    (*a*) Certify the fairness, regularity and consistency of the company's financial statements.
    (*b*) Must verify the fairness of the information given in the directors' report.
    The general report normally comments on the board's proposals for profit distribution and must report any irregularities or inaccuracies that the auditor has found.
2   The special report which deals exclusively with contracts or agreements between the company and any of its directors (or any concerns with which the directors are connected) and must state:
    (*a*) Whether the contracts were approved in advance by the board.
    (*b*) How the company is affected by them.

Latterly, L'Ordre has recommended a standard form of auditor's report which refers to generally accepted auditing standards, the carrying out of verifications in accordance with rules of normal diligence, and the application of generally accepted accounting principles. However, these standards must be interpreted within the confines of government legislation, the Plan Comptable, and the tax rules available for mitigating liability.

The directors also must report annually in a manner common to all countries' boards of management. This report must be certified by the auditor with regard to the financial information which it contains. It will also refer to the directors' remuneration – normally in the form of a percentage of profits and termed a 'tantieme' – and the remuneration and travelling expenses of the ten highest paid persons, in any company having more than 200 employees.

Accounting

The accounting standards in use are those prescribed by the Plan Comptable, (obligatory by law for the limited company) and positively supported by the tax laws which require accounts to be in the prescribed format. The aims behind the Plan Comptable were largely to ensure the provision of more relevant statistics and national comparability for economic, social and fiscal planning purposes. Devised in 1947, the Plan is currently being revised for the third time in order to make it more realistic to a developing economy. Although highly detailed and rigid in form there are still many areas where, in practice, standards need to be set or methods revised; the fullness of the information contained on the face of the accounts does not compensate for the lack of supplementary information. Details of the information required are included in the summary.

Extra-statutory Requirements

In common with most of the continental countries, the amount of legislation and government control in France leaves little scope for self-regulatory mechanisms. Several factors have combined to give the French Stock Market a low and narrow image:

1 A basic conservatism allied to conservation of assets.
2 The provision of government institutions to fulfil (or at least provide for) firms' financial needs.
3 A history of unstable and secretive financial deals and transactions.

Given, in addition, the French investor's preference for liquidity and physical assets, it becomes clear that nothing short of a change in attitude on the part of the investor will provide much domestic buoyancy to the French Stock Exchange. Although the banks are largely involved in investors' market dealings, they do not have the stranglehold possessed by the German banks; nor is there the same potential conflict of interests. There is, however, a considerable unofficial market which by-passes the official mechanism. One of the main drawbacks of the Paris Bourse is the institutional specialization which limits its comprehensiveness. Most extra-statutory requirements, therefore, stem from the need to increase the attractiveness of the stock market.

Professional Bodies

There is little call for extra-statutory controls in the form of accounting standards because of the prescriptive nature of the Plan Comptable, although in fact there are doubts as to its appropriateness for decision-making at the micro, as distinct from the macro, level. Discussion papers are beginning to appear with regard to auditing problems, but these are still at an early stage.

Stock Exchange

Despite a considerable boom in the French economy and increasing demands by industry for funds, the Stock Exchange is prevented from realizing its potential by the numerous controls exercised over the various institutions by the Government through the Bank of France. However, two events have occurred which have been instrumental in improving the position:

1 The first was the formation, in 1967, of La Commission des Operations de Bourse (COB) or Stock Exchange Commission, which was set up to improve the standing and efficiency of the Paris Stock Market by checking the truth and completeness of information provided. Despite somewhat limited means at its disposal, it has assumed the role of Ombudsman and Law Commission combined and has exercised considerable influence over auditors, security analysts and the financial press. This has been achieved by a vigorous policy of publicity and indoctrination which has included:
    (a) Annual reports on transactions which have been against the spirit of full disclosure of information.

(b) Accounting anomolies arising because of the pressures of tax legislation.

(c) The investigation of the adequacy of the audit work carried out preparatory to the issuing of an audit certificate. These investigations have had the unique result of the occasional removal of incapable auditors.

The COB has also been instrumental in increasing the provision of consolidated accounts by existing quoted companies. The COB has also defined, and achieved a reduction in, insider dealing on the Stock Exchange.

2   The second event was the Baumgartner Commission, instigated by the Minister of Finance to investigate the possibility of reforming the financial institutions. This Commission reported in July 1972 on the structure and functions of the Stock Exchange. It has been suggested that any increase in Stock Market activity inevitably alters the emphasis of financial reporting, and the effect of the Baumgartner Commission's recommendations will be to increase Stock Market activity. Among the recommendations of the report (largely aimed at increasing the attractiveness of share ownership to the French public as well as widening the market generally) were:

(a) The granting of tax credits to foreign investors.

(b) Lower taxes on dividends.

(c) Changes in the stockbroking system (allowing limited liability status and the establishment of 'contrapartistes' or jobbers).

(d) The introduction of block trading of shares to promote institutional business.

(e) Easing of the rules covering new issues.

Some of these recommendations have already been implemented.

Financial reporting requirements Until 1972 there were no requirements as to the provision of consolidated accounts for investors, the provisions of the Plan Comptable regarding information on subsidiaries and associations being relied upon. However, the operations of the COB have resulted in an increase in the number of companies presenting consolidated accounts, and since 1971 no French company is allowed to raise funds on the capital market without issuing consolidated accounts. There is a considerable proliferation of methods used in the preparation of these accounts, not all companies using the recommended rules adopted by the COB, and, unfortunately, there is no requirement for consolidated accounts to be presented in subsequent reports. There is some sign of a gradual improvement in the quality, as distinct from the quantity, of interim financial information presented.

Listing requirements and prospectuses A company requiring a listing must file a document containing information as to the firm's activities, investment plans, subsidiaries and their holdings, and dividends distributed. In addition, financial accounts for the previous ten years, together with directors' reports and minutes of shareholders' meetings for the last five, must be presented. A detailed statement of asset and liability changes over the last three years must also be given. The firm must present consolidated information (as outlined above), and must undertake to publish quarterly financial and turnover information, but there is no requirement for an independent accountant's report.

Takeover and Merger Requirements

There is no system of extra-statutory control regarding takeovers and mergers since most of these operations are subject to Government intervention and control. The Ministry of Finance works in conjunction with the Stock Exchange Council and the COB to regulate takeover activity, and with the COB to control mergers. (Under French law, a merger involves the dissolution of the merged companies). There is a preference for the formation of new businesses rather than the purchase of existing ones.

Summary of the Principal Areas of Current Accounting and Reporting Requirements in France

Accountant's Report Included in a Prospectus for the Sale of Securities

There is no requirement for an independent accountant's report or for an expert opinion on profit forecasts. However, a document must be filed which details the firm's activities, investment plans, subsidiaries and their holding, together with a note of dividends distributed. Financial accounts (consolidated in the case of groups) must be included covering the last ten years, and directors' reports and minutes of shareholders' meetings over the last five years must also be presented. There must also be a detailed statement of changes in assets and liabilities over the last three years. The firm must undertake to publish quarterly financial and turnover information.

Form and Content of Published Accounts

All limited companies, private and public, are required to file copies of the audited balance sheet, profit and loss account and annual report(s) with the local registry within one month of their adoption by the shareholders in annual general meeting. In the case of quoted companies whose total assets exceed Fr 10 million (£900000), the above documents must be published in the official gazette, as also must quarterly interim financial statements and similar information with regard to any subsidiaries of such quoted companies. The information required to be published annually, in addition to the final accounts, includes details of any additional liabilities other than those shown on the face of the accounts, details of profit appropriation, holdings in subsidiary and associated companies, and an inventory of movable securities. The interim information, in addition to a provisional balance sheet, must include details of the company's turnover for the quarter (analysed by industrial activity where appropriate) together with comparative figures of the previous and corresponding quarters. The turnover information must be published within one month of the quarter day, and the provisional balance sheet within three months.

The legal requirements regarding the content and classification of final accounts are contained in the Plan Comptable Generale as supplemented by the 1966 Act and subsequent decrees. The balance sheet shows separately:

1 Unamortized formation and issue expenses.
2 Fixed assets, sub-divided between property, plant, equipment and intangibles on the one hand, and fixed (in excess of one year) loans and investments on the other.
3 Current assets (classifying stocks and other current assets separately).

4   Loss for the year, if applicable.
5   Guarantees received.
6   Capital (distinguishing called up from uncalled capital).
7   Reserves, differentiating between legal, statutory, other specific reserves and pro-
    visions.
8   Liabilities, separating long-term (over one year) from others.
9   Profit for the year.
10 The amount of any guarantees given.

Valuation rules are also contained in the Plan Comptable. The profit and loss account is
shown in account form and includes a trading section which must differentiate between
sales and income from other sources, trading and other items (including depreciation and
provisions), and exceptional items, taxes and losses relating to earlier years. Details of the
profit distribution are not included in the profit and loss section and appropriations are
not normally separated from the bulk of the expense items. Analyses of fixed assets and
depreciation, schedules of short-term and long-term gains and analyses of reserves are all
required for tax return purposes, but are only seldom included with the published
accounts. Notes and supplementary information regarding items in the accounts are
rare. There is no legal requirement for the publication of consolidated statements in
France, although a holding company must, at least, publish a statement showing net
income, sales and parent company equity of all its first tier subsidiaries. A similar statement must be published for all those companies where 10% or more of the equity capital
is held. The Plan Comptable prohibits equity accounting for investments. Despite the
COB requirements for consolidated accounts to be presented in relation to new issues,
there is no similar requirement covering subsequent, annual reporting.

The auditor must certify the fairness, regularity, and consistency of the company's balances, financial statements and the directors' report insofar as it concerns the financial
statements. In addition, the auditor must report any irregularities or inaccuracies found.
The certification and the statement as to irregularities constitute the general report. He
must also submit a special report dealing exclusively with contracts or agreements between the company and any of its directors or concerns with which they are connected,
which must state the effect of the contracts or agreements on the company and whether
they had been approved in advance by the board. The general report is usually in long
form and contains comments on the recommended profit distribution. No standard form
of report exists although L'Ordre is currently suggesting that a standard form be adopted
which refers to generally accepted auditing standards, accounting principles and rules of
normal diligence in the carrying out of verifications.

The directors' report would normally refer to the company's financial and profit position, although there is little statutory requirement because of the rules as to financial
statements prescribed by the Plan Comptable, the 1966 Act and the tax legislation. It
refers to the directors' remuneration which, when in the form of a 'tantieme', (share of
profits) is only permitted where a dividend is being paid to shareholders. It must also
refer to the travelling expenses of the ten highest paid persons in any company employing
more than 200 persons. The directors would also normally recommend profit distributions for the shareholders' authorization.

Current Practice

Fixed assets The basis on which fixed assets are valued is not normally disclosed even though it is frequently not historical cost in the case of those assets acquired before 1959. Up to 1959 the Government decreed that larger companies must, and smaller companies could (and most did), revalue their fixed assets in accordance with published price-level indexes. Such revaluations were to be credited to a reserve which could be capitalized or distributed where they were considered to be realized. Depreciation (termed amortization) prior to 1960 had to be provided on the straight-line basis on the higher values, any accumulated provisions being recalculated according to the relevant indexes. In 1960 the reducing balance method was recognized and made permissible for tax purposes. Since the tax legislation only recognizes items charged in the financial accounts, most firms changed to the reducing balance method in order to obtain maximum advantage in the early years. Although firms must now charge depreciation within the parameters of straight-line or reducing balance, even in loss years, it is regarded as permissible to change from one to the other in order to give a lesser charge in such years, reverting to the original method in subsequent years. Such changes are unlikely to be disclosed. Excessive depreciation may also be charged – in accordance with tax legislation – because of the depreciation bearing little relationship to the asset's effective life. Figures are to be shown at cost or adjusted value and the accumulated depreciation together with any reserves for loss in value are deducted to arrive at book value.

Goodwill and intangibles Intangibles generally must be written off against profits in the year in which incurred unless they result in some tangible asset in which case they are written off according to the rules applicable to that particular class of asset. In loss years, expenditure on intangibles may be placed to 'frais d'etablissement' – an asset account – to be written off as soon as profits are available, or within five years, whichever is the less.

Investments Investments are not normally divided into subsidiaries and affiliates on the one hand and general investments on the other. Loans due after a period longer than a year are separated. The basis of valuation is the lower of cost or net realizable value. Those held prior to 1959 were revalued according to specified price level indexes. Again, tax law permits allowable write-downs provided that such provisions are 'booked' in the financial accounts.

Current assets and stocks These are normally valued at the lower of cost or net realizable value. Since tax law does not recognize provisions against doubtful debts until such debts are known to be irrecoverable, debtors are not written down until they can be written off. Stocks are also normally valued on the lower of cost or market method, although, again, such terms are prescribed by the tax laws. Cost includes adjustments for any significant price change and also includes overheads. Any such reserves for replacement or price level changes are shown on the liabilities side of the balance sheet. Since tax laws allow the average flow system and preclude FIFO and LIFO, the former method is utilized for valuing purposes.

Deferred charges The rules relating to deferred charges are such that they must be written off in the year in which they are incurred or carried forward as an asset in the balance sheet to be written off over five years, or earlier if the company is profitable.

Liabilities Liabilities are differentiated on the basis of those which are long-term (maturity more than one year hence) and short-term (others). The latter are shown in considerable detail.

Reserves and provisions A legal reserve of at least 10% of the par value of the share capital has to be maintained and, until it reaches this proportion, 5% of net profits must be appropriated annually. This reserve may only be used to compensate an accumulated loss. A share premium account is not restricted as to use and may be retained, capitalized or distributed as dividend. A company's articles may require particular reserves known as statutory reserves. Equipment Subsidy Reserves are brought into being on receipt of Government subsidies and released to income over the life of the assets to which they relate. Optional reserves are the appropriations of profits authorized by the shareholders for distribution as dividend. Other reserves are listed in specific detail. Reserves for losses and charges is the heading given to provisions for such items as pending litigation, future plant closure costs or other contingencies. Such provisions may be large and may or may not be referred to in the directors' report. Secret reserves are quite common arising from excessive write-downs of fixed assets in particular, and the over-provision for contingencies. It is not normal practice, nor required by law, to show movements on reserves.

Share capital All shares must have a par value and may be in the form of bearer shares but a company cannot normally purchase its own shares. At least 25% of share capital must be paid up on issue and the balance paid within five years. Shareholders' equity is not subtotalled and profit/loss is separated from the capital section. Losses are invariably shown on the assets side of the balance sheet and uncalled capital is often treated in a similar manner. Bonus issues are made at par and dividends (proposed) are part of the optional reserves.

Accounting for acquisitions and mergers The pooling of interests method in respect of mergers is not practised in France.

Income statement It is normal to present a trading section as well as a profit and loss account. Turnover is shown, although there are no requirements for it to be analysed, apart from quoted companies which have to differentiate by activity, and often sales are shown gross of VAT. Cost of sales often cannot be ascertained. Depreciation must be shown, although as mentioned in the section on fixed assets, it is not necessarily provided on a consistent basis, and is likely to be calculated according to the permissiveness or otherwise of the tax legislation. The amount of wages and salaries are shown, although the classification of these items is frequently unhelpful for analysis purposes. Charges for interest and provisions are shown but may not be differentiated and this applies also to income generally. Exceptional items are required to be shown. Taxation accounting is practised in France because of the required similarity of 'book' and tax deductions. Occasionally discrepancies arise owing to the use of an accrual concept in the accounts and the use of a cash basis for tax purposes, but these are usually not of material amount. Consequently a deferred system of accounting for tax is not used. Appropriations are not separately distinguished from the current year's items and would include the directors' tantieme or bonus in the optional reserves.

Other points Accounting policies followed are not stated in the accounts since they tend to be implicit in the rules of the Plan Comptable. They are generally based on concepts of the going-concern, matching and, particularly, conservatism, but not necessarily consistency, even though this latter concept is recommended. Consistency is deemed to have been attained provided that the parameters of the tax regulations have not been broken. Notes are often included describing contingent liabilities and supplementary analyses are beginning to appear including fixed assets, depreciation and other reserves. Material post-date events are seldom disclosed nor are capital commitments. Comparative figures are usually given.

Current Trends

The main trend is the attempt to improve the efficiency of the French capital market and to stimulate the role played by the Stock Exchange in encouraging an increase in participation by both institutions and private individuals. Efforts are also being made to strengthen the various institutions themselves in order that they can take a more dynamic role in financial affairs. These moves can be seen in a number of fields, some of which are listed below.

Statutory Trends

In the area of improving the quality of information for investors, a further revision of the Plan Comptable is being undertaken with a view to its development and adaptation to cope with current pressures. In addition, the Government intends to introduce legislation requiring all quoted companies to publish consolidated annual accounts and quarterly turnover figures. The proposed legislation will probably result in a prescribed set of procedures effecting consolidation for the whole of a group.

In order to increase Stock Market activity, the Baumgartner Report recommendations are gradually being implemented, and should help to stabilize market conditions. This should dispense with the unsatisfactory image of the Stock Exchange as being little better than a lottery. Further improvements are promised regarding the law on brokers, the protection of investors, the issue of 'no par value' shares, the contents and frequency of company reports and the establishment of a market code of conduct. Finally, the legislation concerning the compulsory distribution of employees' 'participation' shares is likely to promote some stimulation in individual stock market participation once such shares become transferable.

Professional Trends

There has been a marked increase in moves to improve auditing and accounting standards at the professional level. A number of discussion papers have been issued and conferences arranged in technical auditing, accounting and professional practice matters. Increased information required by tax laws is likely to lead eventually to a duplication for financial reporting purposes.

Other Trends

The COB has stated its intention to work towards the eventual reservation of quoted company audits to the Expert Comptable. This move, combined with the COB's demonstrated intention of publicizing and prohibiting incompetent auditors, is likely to improve the standing of the profession generally, and to promote the raising of auditing standards in particular.

With the prescriptive requirements of the Plan Comptable, the French accounting system exemplifies Mueller's 'uniform approach' described in Chapter 1. In addition, the aims underlying the Plan Comptable, and the insistence that financial reports should conform with the tax legislation, firmly set this uniform system within a macroeconomic framework.

8

Germany

Type of Business Unit

Companies with Limited Liability

Such companies are controlled by the Corporation Act of 1937 as amended, and in the case of public limited companies superceded, by the Corporation Act 1965 (Aktiengesetz). These Acts broadly correspond with the UK Companies Acts although their requirements are much more detailed and prescriptive than those in the UK. Business units with limited liability are comprised of:

1 Public companies (Aktiengesellschaft – AG) which have unlimited right of share transfer, at least five members, a minimum share capital of DM 100000 (approximately £17000), a minimum par value per share of DM 50 (£8), two independent governing bodies – the Vorstand (board of directors or management) and the Aufsichsrat (supervisory board controlling the management). They must publish annual audited accounts together with an audited directors' report and a supervisory board report.

2 Private companies (Gesellschaft mit beschrankter Haftung – GmbH) which have a minimum subscribed capital of DM 20000 (£3300), a minimum individual subscription of DM 500 (£83) and additional units in multiples of DM 100 (£17). They rarely issue shares and have the right to restrict transfer of interests. Although members' liability is restricted to their total subscribed capital, each member is liable for a proportion of any member's unpaid subscription. There must be at least two incorporators but membership may subsequently fall to one; there is no upper limit to the

number of members. In common with all other large enterprises (known as 'capital' companies) regardless of the type of organization, the GmbH has to file annual audited accounts together with the auditor's certificate. A 'large enterprise' is one which meets two of the following criteria: annual sales exceed DM 250 million (£42 million); net assets exceed DM 125 million (£21 million); average number of employees is 5000.

Cooperatives

Cooperatives are legal entities used for communal projects, construction, etc. They may be limited – (Genossenschaft mit beschrankter Haftung – eGmbH) where members' liability is limited to the amount of capital stated in the articles of association; or unlimited (Genossenschaft mit unbeschrankter Haftung – eGmuH).

Partnerships

Partnerships may be:

1   General (Offene Handelsgesellschaft – OHG) which is the normal commercial form but with a separate legal entity in German law.
2   Limited (Kommanditgesellschaft – KG) with at least one general partner.
3   Limited including a GmbH (GmbH & Co) with the GmbH as the general partner although the company maintains its overall limited liability.
4   Limited with shares (Kommanditgesellschaft auf Aktien – KGaA) shareholders have limited liability but there are also unlimited partners. Such partnerships are governed by the Corporation Acts.
5   Silent (Stille Gesellschaft – SG) which is in the form of a joint venture, all partners sharing profits, one of their number being elected to manage the venture.

Sole Traders with Unlimited Liability

A sole trader has unlimited liability unless he is a one-man GmbH as described under private companies with limited liability.

Branches of Foreign Enterprises

A branch of a foreign enterprise must obtain a licence to set up in Germany and must register in the district within which it is established. It has no fixed or minimum capital and its liabilities are those of the foreign parent company.

Business Records

The Commercial Code requires that each business keeps records in a living language (not necessarily German), in bound form (not maintained in practice), and suitable – in the words of the 1965 Corporate Act – to conform 'to the principles of orderly book-keeping'.

The Accounting Profession

Accounting in Germany is undertaken by Wirtschaftsprufer (WP) whose position and profession is protected by law in the Wirtschaftspruferordnung of 1961. This law set up the Wirtschaftspruferkammer, or Chamber, to regulate the profession, to amalgamate the oldest body of public accountants – Vereidigte Buchprufer (VBP) – with the Wirtschaftsprufer, dating from 1931, and to delegate the technical, practising matters to the Institut der Wirtschaftsprufer. The title of WP is restricted to those qualified *and* in practice; a WP who ceases to practise, say to enter business or commerce generally, loses the title and may have to submit himself for reexamination if he subsequently wishes to practise again.

The 1961 Act also licensed the profession of tax adviser (Steuerberater – StB) and tax assistant (Steuerbevollmachtiger – St Bev). It is likely that these two qualifications will eventually be amalgamated, although at present the qualification requirements for StB are much more analogous to those of the WP subject to the obvious specialization in the field of taxation, than those required for StBev which are much less onerous. Many practitioners hold the dual qualifications of WP and StB because of the overlap in the areas of work carried out.

At the end of 1972 there were approximately 3200 WP, some of whom would also rank among the 5300 StB, and a further 22000 StBev. Only a WP can audit the AG, KGaA, the larger GmbH, insurance companies, banks, savings institutions, cooperatives and public utilities, about 30000 entities in all. Of these entities, about 550 are quoted AGs with a total market capitalization of £13300 million at 30 June 1971, and a further 120 large enterprises – mostly GmbH companies – are also subject to statutory audit. There were approximately 80000 GmbH companies at the end of 1970, most of which would voluntarily use the services of WP in some capacity. Unlike in the UK, a WP can practise as an AG or a GmbH provided that the management of such firms are resident WPs even if the shareholders are not. The shares of a WP–AG cannot be listed on a stock exchange but mixed practices of WP and lawyers or StB are allowable. A WP in business on his own account as a sole practitioner cannot operate from more than two offices and a WP cannot employ more than five professional assistants.

The normal method of qualifying as a WP is to graduate in economics, law, engineering or agriculture before obtaining six years' business experience (at least four of which are with a WP, or two with a WP and two with some other professional eg a StB or lawyer), and passing the Institute's professional examinations. These consist of papers in mercantile, public, company and tax law, business economics, auditing, accounting and professional ethics, and include a thesis and an oral examination. Alternatively, a nongraduate can qualify as a WP if he has obtained at least ten years' experience with a WP before presenting himself for the professional examinations. The qualifying requirements for a StB are of a similar nature subject to the specialization in taxation theory and practice. It is unlikely that a person can be admitted as a WP before age 30, although 35 is the usual age at which a student becomes a fully licensed practitioner. Because of the requirement that a WP must be in practice, together with the arduous manner in which qualification must be obtained, it is a career which requires considerable dedication on the part of the student.

   The WP is engaged, in addition to the growing demands for statutory auditing work, on investigations, business and tax consultancy work, executorship and trustee work, asset and company valuations, and the rendering of legal advice of a relevant, business nature. A WP would not undertake bookkeeping, company registrar or secretaryship work. There is a detailed Code of Ethics formulated by the Wirtschaftspruferkammer governing the conduct, rights and duties of a WP, and according to which he can be penalized or excluded from the profession for violating the Code. Professional insurance is required by law, and a fee scale is in operation for statutory audits, the fee being based on a combination of time spent and the amount of total assets owned by the company being audited. The Code also places great stress on the WP's independence, issuing rules as to compatible and incompatible occupations and relationships, and requiring him to take an oath on admission concerning the exercise of his professional duties and responsibilities.

Statutory Requirements

As previously outlined at the beginning of this chapter, the German equivalent to the UK Companies Acts are the Corporation Acts of 1937 and, more importantly, 1965. These acts supplement the German Commercial Code, the 1965 Act superceding the 1937 Act in the case of 'capital' companies. This distinction between 'capital' (equivalent to the proposed UK 'stewardship' company described in 'Current Trends' in Chapter 4) and 'personal' (comparable with the proposed UK 'proprietory' company) companies is interesting because although the former account for less than 10% of the number of firms and approximately one third of all employees, they are typical of the developing organization within an industrially advanced economy. 'Capital' companies consist of the AG and the large GmbH types of organization, as defined at the beginning of this chapter.

   The Stock Exchange Law requires only the publication of accounts, auditor's report, and company history in certain circumstances. The current position as regards statutory requirements relating to the filing and publication of accounts and the disclosure of information is set out in the summary below.

Standards

Auditing

Professional auditing standards are not codified but are laid down or clarified in a series of Institute pronouncements, Wirtschaftspruferkammer regulations or professional literature. The Institute has published a number of opinions and statements (analogous to the ICAEW's 'recommendations') covering such matters as audit objectives, systems of internal control, etc. The function of the auditor is to report solely on the compliance with the law of the financial statements and the report of management. There is no expression of opinion as to the fairness of the accounts presented, nor as to the compliance with accepted business or accounting principles since these 'principles' are spelled out in the 1965 Corporation Act. This act lists the valuation methods and principles to be used – at least within defined minimum as well as maximum limits – and also decrees, in detail, the format of the final accounts. It is possible for different standards to be applied to the accounts of those organizations which do not have to undergo a statutory audit since they are governed in principle by the Corporation Act of 1937. However, there is, in practice, a tendency to adopt the terms of the 1965 Act voluntarily. The auditor, in reporting on the accounts following a statutory audit, is thus confined to stating a fact, namely that the legal requirements have been met. Since the 1965 Act requires that the accounts 'must be drawn up clearly and comprehensively and must, within the limits of the valuation rules, give the clearest possible view of the financial position and the earnings of the company', there is possibly some slight justification for considering that the auditor does express 'an opinion' in his report. As outlined earlier, the auditor's impartiality and independence is very much prescribed by the ethical code and is regarded in the last analysis as a state of mind.

Reporting

Standards of reporting are prescribed by law in the Corporation Act 1965 in the case of the AG. There is a standard form of auditor's report which states:

> According to our audit, made in conformity with our professional duties, the accounting, the annual financial statements and the report of the board of management comply with German law and the Company's articles of association.

The WP can only qualify his report according to clearly identified departures from the law or the company's articles. In practice the auditor normally submits a separate long form report with limited circulation. This report is intended for the supervisory board, and as well as the above standard certificate contains detailed analysis of, and information on, certain of the balances in the financial statements. In many respects it is a report on the efficiency of the board of management as a guide to the supervisory board. In addition, where applicable, the auditor must examine and report on the 'dependency report' as described below.

The board of management must produce an annual report, similar to that issued by the UK board of directors, and referring to such matters as remuneration, valuation methods, etc. Also, where a company is controlled by another enterprise, the management of the former company must produce an annual 'dependency report'. Such a report, which is intended to give protection to minority shareholders and creditors, must state whether the company has received full market value for each transaction and, if not, whether the resulting disadvantage has been compensated for in some other way. It can be seen that confirmation of the correctness or otherwise of the 'dependency report' is a somewhat daunting task when it involves, as it may, the identification of 'full market value'.

Accounting

The accounting standards in use, although well developed, are prescribed by statute or by various decisions of the courts. They therefore tend to a uniformity of financial statement format, a limitation on the accounting methods and concepts available as alternatives, and a somewhat rigid approach to information which it is necessary to disclose.

The tendency is to incorporate most of the necessary detail on the face of the accounts rather than to publish a comprehensive set of explanatory notes.

Significant German concepts and practice are summarized below. This summary demonstrates a significant orientation towards creditor protection, accompanied by a strong emphasis on the presentation of information to comply with the tax legislation. The accounts show a conservative assessment of profits.

Extra-statutory Requirements

The German situation is encompassed by such comprehensive legislation that there is little necessity for extra-statutory controls. The German economy has a marked cápitalist orientation with most industrial firms in private hands, but they are much influenced – and to some extent controlled – by the major banks. There is no free capital market on the UK pattern. The official capital market is under state control, but a semi-official market exists which has less rigorous admission requirements. A considerable amount of business is transacted privately, outside the Stock Exchange, largely between banks. All transactions are for cash.

A notable feature of the German economy is the virtual stranglehold on the financial situation held by the banks who:

1   Control the equity and bond markets.
2   Hold important participations in industry.
3   Leave practically no choice to firms as to where they obtain funds.

A further factor in the power of the banks is that they not only deal in securities on their clients' account, ie they are, in fact, stockbrokers, but they deal on their own account as well. There is thus a considerable potential for a conflict of interests. The widespread and pervasive nature of the bank holdings is extended by the fact that a 25.1% equity holding guarantees the right to veto decisions of the company's management. Thus banks can control directly, through voting power, or indirectly, through the appointment of bank representatives on the supervisory board, large sections of industry for comparatively little outlay. The banks are therefore 'insiders' who have all the information they require for decision-making, and there have been no other parties requiring information of this kind. The importance of the banks explains the 'creditor-orientation' of the accounts, noted previously.

The banks, in an attempt to retain their position of autonomy and control, have agreed to refrain voluntarily from using inside information to the detriment of outside investors, and to conduct dealings *through* the market rather than by-passing it. However, there is no system of sanctions, and there is an exclusion clause (requiring clients' approval) which permits the banks to by-pass the market. In the light of the banks' influence this would not, seemingly, be difficult to obtain. Lack of pressure for extra-statutory requirements explains their absence.

Professional Bodies

The accounting profession has issued a number of opinions and statements (see

'Auditing' under 'Standards' above) and these are well-defined. Being recommendations they are not mandatory, but are subject to an on-going process which ensures that they are reasonably in tune with current problems.

Stock Exchange

Financial reporting requirements Certain reporting requirements exist but these are more than covered by the statutory requirements for annual, audited accounts of quoted companies. Despite the lack of Stock Exchange requirements for interim profit figures, these are often provided by the larger groups on a half-yearly or even quarterly basis, in a voluntary, but frequently not consolidated, manner.

Listing requirements and prospectus The granting of a Stock Exchange quotation is subject to legislation contained in the Stock Exchange Act, as amended, and the rules of the Stock Exchange Admissions Office. This office merely ascertains the completeness of the information without investigating its accuracy.

Takeover and Merger Requirements

There are no extra-statutory requirements.

Summary of the Principal Areas of Current Accounting and Reporting Requirements in Germany.

Accountant's Report to be Included in a Prospectus for the Sale of Securities

A prospectus must be issued and published, containing extracts from the articles of the company, the last finalized accounts (which must not be more than 13 months old) and details of the last five years' dividends. Information on the company's activities, investments in other companies, management and future prospects must also be included. The extent of the conditions and rights attaching to the proposed loan or share issue must be stated. The prospectus is the prerogative of the banks and the issuer, the auditor merely certifying the validity and legal correctness of the financial accounts. There is no separate accountant's report, nor any involvement in a profits forecast.

Form and Content of Published Accounts

All public companies, the larger private, limited companies and all banking and insurance companies are required to file an audited balance sheet and profit and loss account, auditor's certificate and annual management report with the local Trade Registry. In addition, the audited financial statements must be published in the Federal Gazette. Any publication of an abbreviated form of the financial statements must not bear the auditor's certificate and must also contain a reference to the fact that the accounts are not shown in full. On enquiry, the company must inform the inquirer as to the issue of the Federal Gazette in which the full accounts appear.

The balance sheet must be prepared according to a prescribed form which classifies fixed assets into tangible fixed, investments, and long-term (five or more years) loans, together with a note of any securities held. Stocks must be shown separately. Other assets must include information designed to clarify the liquid state of debtors and bills receivable, and must distinguish deferred charges. Liabilities must be differentiated between those not due for at least four years (together with the amounts secured by mortgage) and other liabilities, the latter category requiring separation of any pension accruals from long-term accruals generally. Reserves must differentiate between legal, voluntary and asset valuation reserves. Notes must be included of any discounted bills not yet due, suretyships or guarantees entered into. The valuation principles to be used are implied within the 'principles of orderly bookkeeping' variously defined in the Commercial Code and the Corporation Acts.

The profit and loss account must be in report form and is again prescribed as to form and classification. It must state separately:

1   Sales revenue of a genuine nature and related cost of sales.
2   Investment income, classified according to source.
3   Wages and social employment costs.
4   Separately classified depreciation charges.
5   Gains/losses on disposal of fixed assets.
6   Extraordinary items.
7   Interest and taxes.
8   Transfers to reserves, differentiating between legal and voluntary transfers.

A consolidated balance sheet and profit and loss statement must be prepared, together with a group management report, in all cases where a company owns more than 50% of another domestic company's equity share capital. Such group accounts must also be reported on by a WP and must be produced within five months of the parent company's year-end. Majority interests, where they exist, must be notified and, in the case of other affiliations involving 25% or greater equity holding, the legal and business nature of the affiliation must be notified and disclosure made of any claims and liabilities on the balance sheet. Details of share dealings between dependent and/or subsidiary companies must be disclosed in the management report.

In the financial accounts no distinction is made between trade and non-trade indebtedness between affiliates. The inclusion of foreign domiciled affiliated companies in the reports and financial statements of German companies is entirely optional to the domestic company, as also is the consolidation, even of wholly-owned subsidiaries, where such subsidiaries are domiciled outside the Federal Republic of West Germany.

The auditor must certify the accounts and the management report according to a standard short form report. Such a report states that:

> According to our audit, made in conformity with our professional duties, the accounting, the annual financial statements and the report of the board of management comply with German law and the company's articles of association.

Qualifications to the report can only be made in connection with clearly defined departures from law or the company's statutes even though the 1965 Act does require the accounts to be drawn up clearly and comprehensively so that, within the limits of the valuation rules, they give the clearest possible view of the financial position and the earnings of the company. Normally, the auditor will also produce a long form report which contains a detailed analysis of, and information on, certain of the balances in the financial statements as well as the standard short form certificate. The long form report is made to the supervisory board and is not available to the shareholders. The auditor also has to certify the correctness or otherwise of the dependency report. The auditor may be required to attend the directors' meeting considering the annual accounts before they are presented to the shareholders. He must attend the annual general meeting of shareholders if requested to do so by the supervisory board, but may only answer shareholders' questions if he is specifically authorized to do so by the supervisory board.

The report of management to the shareholders is a two part document, dealing with the general situation of the company on the one hand and an explanation of detailed items in the financial statements on the other. The auditor must refer in his report to his general examination and concurrence with the former aspect and his detailed examination and agreement with the latter explanations. The management report must specifically explain the valuation and depreciation methods used in sufficient detail to give a meaningful insight into the company's financial and profit situation and also refer to any material changes from earlier valuations. In this latter connection, the act defines materiality as being anything in excess of either a 10% change in profits, or a 0.5% change in capital stock, whichever is the less. A dependency report must also be prepared, where appropriate, stating whether the company has received full market value for each transaction and, if not, whether the resulting disadvantage to the firm has been compensated for in some other way. This report is aimed at protecting the interests of minority shareholders and creditors. Finally, the report of the supervisory board to the shareholders, would, among other matters, refer to any qualifications to the financial statements or management report resulting from the audit.

Current Practice

Fixed assets Fixed asset values must not exceed historic cost and the recording of unrealized gains is banned. The tendency prior to the 1965 Act of charging excessive depreciation in order to arrive at undervaluations and reduced distributable profit has now been outlawed by that act, whereby depreciation may be charged on those fixed assets that are subject to wear and tear if such depreciation has been calculated according to a plan based on generally accepted principles of accounting. However, in order to benefit from tax legislation such principles will normally include accelerated depreciation which must be recorded in the books. Extraordinary depreciation may be charged where the value of specified fixed assets has fallen below the book value which would be left if only normal depreciation had been charged and, since there is no sanction by management having to write back excessive depreciation in future years, it is still possible to create secret reserves. Figures tend to be shown at book value brought forward without any figure for accumulated depreciation, although movements in fixed asset accounts must be disclosed.

Goodwill and intangibles Goodwill and intangibles can only be recorded as assets if they have been acquired from some other party at a cost, such cost providing the maximum value. Goodwill, once recorded, must be written off through profit and loss account within five years of purchase as a maximum period. Other intangibles must be amortized over their lifetime.

Investments Investments must be split between those in companies, those not due to mature within four years (together with details of security), and others. Where the market value of an individual investment falls below cost, the total of that class must be reduced; it is not possible to offset a loss on one against a rise in value of another.

Current assets and stocks The values of current assets must not be higher than cost or market and may be reduced where management anticipates, using reasonable business judgement, a decline in market prices. Stocks are valued on the above basis, and, in the case of 'strategic raw materials' may be reduced by up to 20% of cost in certain cases allowed by the income tax legislation. Cost is generally deemed to include overheads, although some firms include only direct charges. The flow assumed is a moving average, although FIFO and LIFO methods are acceptable for tax purposes if it can be shown that such methods accord with the facts. Debtors, where doubtful, should be reserved against, and deducted from the asset in the case of known individuals. They should be shown as a 'valuation reserve' on the liabilities side in the case of an overall reserve.

Deferred charges Only those charges specifically identifiable with assets to be used or sold may be carried forward. The general rule is that deferred charges as such be written off to profit and loss account in the year in which they are incurred.

Liabilities Liabilities are divided into long-term (four years and over) and short-term, and details of securities granted must be stated. Certain companies in existence in 1948 are still paying a levy until 1979 based on their net assets at 1948 and such liability may only be shown by way of a note.

Reserves and provisions A legal reserve is required to be maintained of at least 10% of the par value of the share capital and, until it reaches this proportion, 5% of net profits must be appropriated annually. A share premium can form part of this legal reserve which may only be used to cover operating losses or an asset write down. The free reserves, or earned surplus, are partly built up by management discretion and partly by that of the shareholders, as management can stipulate that up to 50% of annual profits must be appropriated to free reserves, subject to an over-riding limit that such reserves, after appropriation, must not exceed 50% of the par value of the share capital, and the shareholders can determine how much of the remaining profits shall be distributed. Secret reserves are commonplace in German accounts although most originated prior to the 1965 Act. Although the Act has imposed minimum as well as maximum values and has stipulated that movements on reserves be disclosed, this has only served to throw a little light on secret reserves; as outlined earlier, in the section on fixed assets, the facilities still exist for a determined management to create secret reserves within the law, particularly when supported by the tax law.

Share capital All shares must have a par value, must value at least DM50 (£8), and may be in the form of bearer shares. The number of authorized shares is disclosed in the narrative rather than on the face of the balance sheet and any unpaid subscriptions on shares appear on the assets side of the balance sheet. A company can purchase its own shares which are shown at par as an asset until cancelled. Any such holding is limited to 10% of the share capital and does not carry voting rights. Shareholders' equity is not shown as a separate sub-total in the model chart of accounts and profit is shown separately. Bonus issues are made at par and dividends are shown as paid, not proposed, the effect of proposals being outlined in the supplementary notes.

Accounting for acquisitions and mergers The main point concerning this matter is that no differentiation is made on an acquisition between pre- and post-acquisition profits. As a result, the figure for goodwill may fluctuate from year to year in accordance with movements on the subsidiaries' reserves. This lack of distinction, particularly when combined with the profits/losses of numerous subsidiaries within a group, completely obscures any informational content.

Income Statement Net sales must be disclosed in the profit and loss statement. Depreciation must be shown, although the amount is likely to be in accordance with the accelerated provisions of tax legislation since only if such amounts are charged in the financial accounts will they be allowed for tax purposes. The total amount of wages and salaries and also social costs are shown. Charges for interest and provisions must be shown as also must any income or loss from subsidiaries and/or affiliates. Extraordinary items must also be shown.

Taxation accounting is practised in Germany because of the requirement that any items, to be allowed, must be charged in the financial accounts. However, despite this 'principle of common basis' there may still be discrepancies between estimated and actual liabilities. As such discrepancies are rarely disclosed, and as the 'book' and 'tax' depreciations seldom disagree, there is no system of deferred accounting for taxation. There is currently a move to introduce an independent balance sheet for taxation purposes but it is understood that this proposal is not included in the Tax Reform Plan for 1974.

Appropriations are separately distinguished and the model form of statement does provide a subtotal purporting to be the result for the period. However, there is no separation of the net operating profit/loss. Where applicable a separate statement showing movements on reserves must be made.

Other points Notes on accounting policies, eg concerning valuations, may be provided for shareholders, and such policies are generally based on concepts of the going-concern, matching and, particularly, conservatism, but not, specifically, consistency. Notes would also be included as to contingent liabilities but not, usually, in respect of capital commitments. Comparative figures are provided and material post-date events must be disclosed.

Current Trends

The system of ownership and control of industry in Germany is now going through a period of almost revolutionary change which will result in increasing pressure for changes in accounting information and disclosure practices. Most of the changes are likely to be statutory.

Statutory Trends

Reforms are likely in the areas of banking, cartels and Stock Exchange activity. Employees' shareholding and financial reporting are also probable areas for legislative reform.

Banking reform There is a strong move towards nationalization of German banks in order to curb their traditional power and to regulate their activities. Such a move fore-shadows:

1 A limitation of banks' stock market dealings.
2 Control over the appointment of bank representatives on supervisory boards.
3 A streamlining of the publicly controlled banking sector.

Cartel legislation The increase in the number of takeovers and mergers, many of them carried out in the utmost secrecy and often engineered by one or two large institutions, has already led to regulatory legislation in August 1973. This legislation is aimed at re-stricting the ability of large institutions and/or major shareholders to push through im-portant amalgamations behind the scenes. It requires the provision and publication of much more detailed information before the operation can be carried through.

Stock Exchange law reform New laws are currently under preparation which will en-courage increased Stock Exchange activity, and will require the provision of further in-formation before a company can obtain a listing. It is thereby hoped to improve the volume of information available to the public about quoted companies.

Employees' shareholding Current moves to implement employees' profit-sharing/'asset building' schemes will, if successful, bring into being a new unit trust type of holding. Such schemes are likely to broaden stock market activity and lead to the pro-vision of information to a new 'interested party' in the long run.

Financial reporting There are proposals to separate tax reporting from financial report-ing. Although accepted in principle for the Tax Reform Plan, these proposals have cur-rently been deferred. If implemented, the proposals will remove the current taxation orientation of financial reporting practice.

Other Trends

The ambitious investment programmes which are being undertaken by many German firms involve a considerable growth in the size of the business unit. The growth is largely manifested by the increasing takeover and merger activity referred to above. Larger units are likely to increase demands for long-term capital which cannot be met by the banks alone. It is likely, therefore, that efforts will be made to expand stock market activity both in the number of firms coming to the market and the number of new investors. Any such expansion is likely to create demands for more investor-orientated financial information.
    The German system of accounting is therefore in a transitional situation. Until the

early 1940s it followed the macroeconomic pattern identified by Mueller described in Chapter 1 and operated within a macroeconomic business environment. Since the mid-1940s, however, the accounting system has been less suitable for the environment in which it operates. Accounting practice has remained rigid and prescribed, whilst its environment has required a more flexible, pragmatic approach to financial reporting.

9

Holland

Type of Business Unit

Companies with Limited Liability.

These companies are controlled by the Netherlands Commercial Code as supplemented by the Act on Annual Accounts of Enterprises 1970, and the Act on Private Limited Liability Companies 1971 together with the Adaptation Act on Private Companies 1971. These Acts, in conjunction with the relevant sections of the Code of Commerce, broadly correspond to the UK Companies Acts 1948 and 1967. Business units with limited liability are comprised of:

1   Public companies (Naamloze Vennootschap – NV) have: unlimited right of share transfer; at least two members on incorporation which may subsequently fall to one; and published, audited annual accounts together with an (unaudited) directors' report.
2   Private companies (Besloten Vennootschap – BV) were brought into being by the 1971 Acts, and cannot issue share certificates – they merely record ownership interests in a register – and restrict the right of transfer of such interests. The larger private companies, ie those with share capital of at least H fl 500 000 (£80 000) or total assets in excess of H fl 8 million (£1.28 million) and more than 100 employees, and certain banking and insurance companies, are required to publish annual audited accounts. As from June 1974 the auditor's report must also be included in the publication.

Cooperatives

These include certain specific types of organization governed by the Act on Annual Accounts of Enterprises or other specific requirements, eg Cooperative Societies (Coöperatieve Vereniging) cooperatives generally, and mutual insurance companies. Co-operatives with assets exceeding H fl 3 million (£480000) must publish financial accounts.

Partnerships

Partnerships may be:

1   General (Vennootschap Onder Firma – VOF) the normal commercial form.
2   Limited (Commanditaire Vennootschap – CV) with at least one general or unlimited partner. Liability of other partners is limited according to subscribed capital.
3   Limited with shares (Commanditaire Vennootschap op Aandelen – CVOA) as 2 above except that the liability of limited partners is represented by transferable shares.
4   Civil (Maatschap) which is a general partnership of professional persons governed by the Civil rather than the Commercial Code.

Sole Trader with Unlimited Liability

Non-resident Enterprises

A non-resident may set up a permanent establishment subject to a licence from the Nederlandsche Bank. A further permit must be obtained from the Ministry of Economic Affairs for investments in general industrial activities. Thereafter there is no discrimination between non-resident and resident companies.

Business Records

The Netherlands Commercial Code merely provides that everyone carrying on a business must keep proper records so that his assets and liabilities may be ascertained at any time.

The Accounting Profession

The accounting profession as currently organized in Holland is an amalgam of the Nederlands Instituut van Accountants (NIvA) formed in 1895, and the Vereniging van Academisch Gevormde Accountants (VAGA) dating from 1927. Until the early 1960s VAGA formed the academic, but not necessarily professionally experienced, section of the Dutch accounting scene. In 1962 the Registered Accountants Act was passed with the intention of restricting the title of 'Registeraccountant' in order to:

1   Safeguard the interests of suitably qualified and experienced accountants.
2   Ensure adequate standards of training and education.

3   Maintain and raise standards of professional performance.

The Act preceded a period of commercial and company law reform in the early 1970s and was followed by the unification of the Dutch accounting profession in the Nederlands Instituut van Registeraccountants (NIvRA) formed in 1967 from the membership of the NIvA and the VAGA. Although there are other organizations of accountants in Holland they are not recognized for purposes of the audit of companies, do not enjoy the same professional exclusivity and are restricted to work of a bookkeeping or tax computational nature.

On 1 September 1972 there were about 3200 members of the NIvRA of whom approximately half were in public practice. These practitioners audited 400 quoted companies with a total market capitalization of £5300 million at 31 December 1971. As in Germany, practitioners are allowed to form limited liability companies and mixed partnerships. However, since this concession dates only from 1973, most are still partnerships (Maatschaps) or sole practitioners. In order to qualify as a registeraccountant a student must obtain the Accountancy Diploma. This may be obtained by way of professional experience and examination or – unlike in the UK – by means of postgraduate study in accountancy following a first degree in economics. The former method takes at least eight years and normally includes three sets of examinations in civil law, mathematics and economics after three and a half years' study, in taxation, advanced economics, accounting and auditing after a further four years, followed by a dissertation on a relevant topic, usually in the field of auditing. There is no requirement for a student to be apprenticed to a registeraccountant and the broadness and theoretical foundation of the NIvRA examination pattern does seem to form a useful base for future flexibility in accounting practice. It also makes the academic method of qualifying a feasible and attractive alternative.

Like his UK Chartered Accountant counterpart, the Dutch Registeraccountant in practice is engaged upon:

1   Investigatory work for company, purchaser and government purposes.
2   Management and tax consultancy work.

Perhaps because of the Dutch concentration on continuity and 'the preservation of the enterprise', the Registeraccountant is seldom called upon to undertake liquidation and receivership. The similarity with the UK Chartered Accountant is strengthened by the presence of a rigorous code of ethics, although in the case of the Registeraccountant the code of ethics was laid down by the Ministry of Economic Affairs following the Registered Accountants Act.

Statutory Requirements

The Dutch Companies Acts supplement the Netherlands Commercial Code Sections 36–56. The 1970 Act largely follows the report of the Verdam Committee (set up in 1960) and was in some respects transitional, although in many other ways anticipatory, pending the harmonization of company law within the EEC. The 1971 Acts were directly anticipatory of the forthcoming company law harmonization rules since they brought into being, for the first time under Dutch law, the close company form of business organization. A notable feature of Dutch company law is the enlightened, active role played by the employers' federations in the formulation and recommendations concerning best practice. The current position in Holland with regard to statutory requirements is included in the summary. In general, legislation governs the filing and publication of company information as in UK.

Standards

Auditing

Professional auditing standards are not codified, but guidelines are contained in the 'Rules on Professional Activities of Register Accountants' promulgated by the Ministry of Economic Affairs and stemming from the rules of the earlier NIvA and VAGA. As in the UK, the emphasis is on the auditor using those standards which he regards to be necessary. He must provide information which reflects the state of the company's affairs 'fairly and systematically', in such a manner as to permit the forming of 'sound judgement' on the affairs, insofar as annual accounts permit this to be done. He must ensure that the underlying bases comply with those standards regarded as being acceptable 'in economic and social life'. Noncompliance with the Act on Financial Statements must be specifically reported on by the auditor. The Code of Ethics and the Rules both stress the need for the auditor to be impartial and independent.

Reporting

No standard form of auditors' report exists and a 'clean' report implies unqualified affirmation of the documents reported upon, the information and notes relating thereto, and the fulfilment of the standards outlined above. The report refers to the profit and loss account – and appropriation section, if one is included – as well as to the balance sheet and accompanying notes. It does not relate to any report of the management or board of directors, and thus the accounts and accompanying notes are intended to provide all necessary information. Although, in some instances, the auditors' 'report' merely states 'audited and approved' there is a strong move towards the establishment of a clear and unambiguous short form of audit report which could be generally adopted.

The board of directors or executive managers must report annually to the shareholders in the case of an NV or the larger BV. This report, preferably although not necessarily in writing, deals with the course of affairs of the company and the managing director's stewardship. The report is definitely distinguished from the audited accounts and the contents are not statutorily defined.

Accounting

There is no formally established code of accounting principles, the obligation throughout being that such principles should be 'in accordance with good commercial practice'. However, this does not imply that high standards do not exist, particularly in larger companies. The 1970 Act on Financial Statements requires compliance with standards that are 'acceptable by the business community' as a minimum for accounting reports (see 'Auditing' above). The business community has taken a considerable and continuing interest in the establishment of standards, a pattern unique in the history of developing accounting standards. A committee composed of entrepreneurs, stock exchange experts, bankers, financial journalists and auditors, under the auspices of the Netherlands Employers' Association, reported in 1955 on the standards which an annual report should meet. In 1962 a second report, 'Reporting, Rendering of Account and Information by the Boards of Limited Liability Companies', was produced by the Association. This report updated the 1955 Report, and also broadened the scope of suggestions to include such matters as the adequacy of existing statutory requirements and the avoidance of rigidity in government regulations. A joint study group of employers' organizations, trade unions and NIvRA are currently compiling a list of acceptable financial reporting standards.

The most significant concepts and practice within the Dutch system of accounting are summarized below.

Extra-statutory Requirements

Compared with the UK, Holland is much more in line with the general continental practice of legislating its requirements rather than leaving whole areas under the voluntary control of various quasi-statutory bodies. However, this does not imply that the Dutch system is in any way rigid. Indeed, the lack of extra-legal requirements is probably due to the fact that flexible legislation has been so recently devised in the light of current needs. The 1970 Act on Annual Accounts of Enterprises sets forth minimum requirements only, and specifically allows for additional information to be supplied where necessary to give a satisfactory insight into a company's financial position.

Professional Bodies

There are no mandatory standards issued by the accounting profession in Holland, but as was seen above and is also described under 'Current trends', there are currently moves to establish an inventory of acceptable standards.

Stock Exchange

The apparent lack in Holland of extra-statutory requirements concerning Stock Exchange information stems from two main factors. Firstly, as mentioned above, legislation has recently been enacted which imposes statutory requirements on quoted companies regarding published financial information. Secondly, the current state of the Dutch stock market is such that it has not been pressurised to anything like the extent of the larger, more equity-conscious UK market.

Although the dealing methods of the Amsterdam Stock Exchange are broadly similar to those of the London Stock Exchange – involving a broker/jobber-type transaction and high voluntary standards – there the similarity ends. The Dutch market is dominated by six Dutch international companies whose standard of reporting is generally in the forefront of best practice. Apart from these companies, capital requirements are almost always met by private loans rather than debentures, or by internal financing. Consequently there is a marked lack of new issues and, in fact, a decline in the amount of trading, evidenced by a 50% fall in the number of local funds dealt in on the stock market over the last decade. A newer feature of the Dutch capital market is the increasing role being played by the institutions, such as pension funds, which are tending to create a closed market between themselves and the state and/or industry. A unique situation – for continental capital markets, at least – is the comparatively small role played by the banks, generally restricted to short-term lending, as the banks are not significantly concerned in the ownership of firms. To date, therefore, there has been little need for the Stock Exchange to improve reporting standards since the 'climate' has largely been set by deals in the shares of firms which are already following acknowledged best practice. In general, the requirements of the Stock Exchange regarding published information over and above the statutory requirements are laid down as a condition of obtaining a quotation by the Stock Exchange Society (Vereeniging voor den Effectenhandel).

Financial reporting requirements Since July 1971 the Stock Exchange Society has required interim financial statements to be published at least half-yearly as a condition of being quoted on the Amsterdam Stock Exchange. Such reports must be published not later than the third and ninth months respectively of the financial year and, interestingly, the reports are still required notwithstanding the fact that shares are placed outside the Stock Exchange. There is no requirement that such statements should be audited but it is implicit in the Stock Exchange rules that the company's registeraccountant has a general professional responsibility over the appropriateness of the accounting principles underlying the statements. There are no requirements regarding group consolidated accounts, although in practice most of the firms supplying interim statements give consolidated figures as part of their operating results. Most of the interim information given is confined to significant operating items such as revenues, depreciation and interest, although some firms also give financial ratios.

Listing requirements and prospectuses The Stock Exchange Society requires that a prospectus must be issued offering shares or debentures to the public, and details of the contents are outlined in the summary. The auditor's consent to his certificate being included must be given in writing, but in cases where accounts have not previously been subject to statutory audit, such a requirement can be waived. There is no requirement for a profit forecast to be included in the prospectus.

Takeover and Merger Requirements

An acceptable code of practice in takeovers and mergers is largely contained in the various enactments and rules contained in the Commercial Code and the Works Councils Acts. Before any bid is made, negotiations with the trade unions concerned must be conducted, and subsequently the motives behind the bid must be made public. However, there are few rules concerning share dealings and there is nothing, for example, to prevent an offeree company issuing shares to a favoured offeror company, provided that no legal relationship exists between the parties at the time.

Summary of the Principal Areas of Current Accounting and Reporting Requirements in Holland

Accountant's Report to be Included in a Prospectus for the Sale of Securities

A prospectus must be issued containing an analysis of the firm's capital and free reserve accounts since its inception. Also, audited balance sheets and income statements for the last two financial years should be included, together with current financial details to the date of the prospectus. The auditor's consent to his certificate being included must be given in writing. Where accounts have not previously been subject to statutory audit, such a requirement is waived. There is no requirement for a profit forecast to be included in the prospectus.

Form and Content of Published Accounts

All public, and larger private, limited companies and all financial and insurance companies must file a copy of their audited balance sheet, profit and loss account, explanatory notes thereto and the auditors' report with the Office of the Trade Register. (The auditors' report pertaining to the larger BV becomes obligatory only in respect of accounts covering the 29 June 1974, or later). Filing must be carried out within eight days of the passing of the accounts in general meeting. Copies of the accounts and auditors' report are made available to the shareholders for inspection, at no cost, at the registered office of the company during the minimum period of 15 days' notice convening the meeting.

The balance sheet must show fixed and intangible assets separately classified, the former valued according to economically and socially acceptable standards, the latter at cost less accumulated amortization. (The bases used are to be disclosed together with the effect, if significant, of any changes therein). The following must be shown:

1 'Fair values' of holdings of at least 25% of issued share capital of other enterprises.
2 A note of any changes in value and the total amount receivable from subsidiaries.
3 The name and domicile of any majority-held subsidiary and other associated firms where the shareholding exceeds 15% of the associated company's issued share capital.

The stock categories and the current assets must be stated separately, together with a note of any irrecoverable debts and the extent of any assets which are not freely disposable. Separate classification must be made, and details shown, of:

1 Issued and paid up capital, the nominal value of repurchased but uncancelled shares and the value at which they are included in the balance sheet, and of any special rights or options attaching to certain shareholders.
2 Reserves, together with any significant movements therein.
3 Liabilities, according to whether they exceed one year's term and/or are secured, and the nature of securities and assets concerned.
4 Any convertible or unexpired items and sureties or guarantees entered into.

The profit and loss account must show details of the scale of business, according to accepted standards, which includes expressing it as a ratio. Emoluments of the joint supervisory directors divided between fixed and other amounts, together with the number of remunerated and unremunerated directors must be shown. Separate details must also be given of:

1   Wages and social costs incurred.
2   Depreciation according to separate classifications.
3   Profits/losses on associated holdings, subsidiaries and investments.
4   Interest.
5   Extraordinary items.
6   Appropriations of profit and treatment of losses, where not explained in the supporting notes.

Consolidated statements are required to be shown, although not necessarily in the form of consolidated accounts. The minimum requirements for group accounts are the accounts of the holding company plus the accounts of the subsidiaries, the latter being prepared for individual subsidiaries or for amalgamations of some or all of them. Such subsidairies' accounts may be shown in the supporting notes and information to the accounts of the holding company. Varying degrees of disclosure are required for investments in associated companies according to whether the degree of control falls within the bands of 15–25%, 25–50%, or is otherwise material.

There is no standard form of auditor's report, but a 'clean' report implies unqualified affirmation of the balance sheet, profit and loss account and any appropriation section, and the accompanying notes. It is normally presented in short form and, as it is now (from June 1974) an obligatory part of the published accounts, it must state whether the accounts fulfil their purpose, and refer specifically to any divergence from statutory provisions. There is now a standard wording for a 'clean' short form of auditor's report. Where a supervisory board exists the auditor reports to such a board rather than to the members. The directors or executive managers must report annually to the shareholders although there is no standard form of reports, nor any statutory requirements, other than that such reports shall be distinguished from, and not considered part of, the annual accounts reported on by the auditors. The report of the managing directors and of the supervisory board may be made orally, but if written, as is more usual, it must be filed and made available to interested parties in the same manner as the annual accounts. The report normally deals with the course of affairs of the company and recommends the appropriations and distributions of profit to the members. A supervisory board has the power to approve or reject the annual audited accounts of the company before they are submitted to the members in general meeting.

Current Practice

Fixed assets Fixed assets are valued basically at historic cost although a number of larger companies have consistently used current values and disclosed the basis in a note. Any differences arising on current valuation are placed to, or less frequently charged against, a revaluation reserve. The additional depreciation charged should be distinguished from that based on cost, and tax legislation does not allow such increased charge. Figures are shown at gross cost, or current value, less accumulated depreciation.

Cost of land tends not to be separated from that of buildings.

Goodwill and intangibles These should be shown according to type and may be retained in the balance sheet at cost less amortization, or written off against income. Use of current values, of course, tends to eliminate much of the goodwill which would otherwise arise on acquisitions.

Investments Those of a marketable nature should be separated from other investments and so also should long-term loans and advances.

Current assets and stocks Current assets as such are not distinguished from fixed assets, the separation being between liquid and illiquid assets. Any fall below cost would normally be provided or noted. Stocks are valued at either the 'lower of cost or market' or at current values, cost usually includes overheads and is usually based on FIFO flow. However, base stock, average and LIFO methods may be used. Disclosure of the basis of cost is not normally made, unless current value is used.

Deferred charges These may be carried forward and amortized over the life of the issue, although frequently written off against income in the year in which they are incurred.

Liabilities Liabilities are distinguished between short-and long-term and different classes of liability. Separate disclosure is required for material long-term commitments (long leases, etc).

Reserves and provisions Distinction is made in the balance sheet between provisions and reserves, the former being divided between short- and long-term, the latter being classified according to whether they represent paid in surplus, retained earnings or reserves arising from revaluations. Provisions are charges against profits for known liabilities, reserves are appropriations of profit. Secret reserves are not a normal feature of Dutch financial statements, although some of the smaller companies may undervalue stocks. However, in the context of European accounting systems generally, secret reserves are nonexistent. There is no requirement, as in many European countries, for a legal reserve.

Share capital All shares must have a par value and may be registered or bearer shares. A company may purchase its own shares and thus the par value of repurchased but uncancelled shares must be shown. The shareholders' equity is normally shown as a subtotal. Bonus issues are made at par value out of either paid in surplus or retained earnings. Details of any options on shares must be stated. Dividends are shown in the accounts as paid, rather than proposed, and may be appropriated in the profit and loss account or in the explanatory notes.

Accounting for acquisitions and mergers Most practice has centred around full-cost accounting for acquisitions and a significant factor is that where current values are used on the acquisition this, of course, eliminates much of the goodwill that would otherwise arise.

Income statement Details regarding sales must be stated although these may take the form of a percentage or index related to the previous year's figures if it is desired not to show absolute amounts. Depreciation must be specifically shown, normally being calculated according to the straight-line or reducing balance method. The charge for depreciation in the financial accounts is unlikely to coincide with that allowed for tax purposes. The total amount of wages and salaries as well as social charges are normally disclosed, together with the management and supervisory board remuneration unless this is in the form of a bonus, which may then be shown as an appropriation of profit. Charges for interest and provisions must be shown as also must any income or loss from subsidiaries. Extraordinary items must also be shown or noted.

Taxation accounting is not practised in Holland and consequently considerable differences can arise between tax as computed on profits and actual liability. Quite frequently a separate set of accounts drawn up in conformity with tax legislation is submitted to the revenue authorities. Deferred taxation entries, although not in general use, are becoming increasingly common in the case of the larger companies in order to cope with the timing discrepancies between recorded and actual taxation liabilities.

Appropriations are recommended to be shown separately from profit determination as well as being individually distinguished, and in many cases this is now done. Where applicable a separate statement showing movements on reserves must be made.

Other points Notes as to earnings per share and accounting policies are often given, such policies generally being based upon going-concern, matching, consistency and prudence concepts. In a number of cases statements of sources and applications of funds and financial and activity ratios are also provided as supplementary information. Comparative figures must be shown and material post-date events and the effect of changes in accounting policies are also disclosed.

Current Trends

The main trend in the Dutch accounting system, other than the gradual implementation of the recent financial reporting requirements, is the move towards compiling an inventory of acceptable standards. This move was instigated by the Minister of Economic Affairs during the parliamentary discussions preparatory to the 1970/71 company legislation.

Statutory Trends

The Government has promised to restrict the use of the title 'accountant' as from 1978 in order to strengthen and protect the accounting profession.

Professional Trends

The tripartite study group described under 'Accounting' in the section on standards, has as its objective the compilation of an inventory of acceptable business and reporting standards. The standards are those used in economic and social life, which, in the opinion of the study group, 'might be deemed acceptable in the present social system'. The operation is analagous to the UK system of exposure drafts and SSAPs. To date, the group has issued two publications for discussion. The first, issued in December 1971, dealt with shareholdings, stocks and liabilities, and was adopted as a definitive statement of standards in July 1974. The second, issued in April 1973, dealt with fixed asset valuations, debtors, capital and provisions, and has not yet been adopted as definitive. The current value basis of fixed asset valuation recommended in the report is likely to result in an increase in the proportion of Dutch quoted companies (currently 15%) who already use this basis in their published accounts.

The system of financial reporting as commonly practised in Holland (at least in the case of the larger quoted companies) contains most of the characteristics of the micro-economic approach identified by Mueller described in Chapter 1. Not only has the business community supported such an accounting orientation but Government also has given statutory recognition in its implementing legislation, both to the respectability of the accountant's role and to the need to preserve a flexible approach to changing conditions.

10

Italy

Type of Business Unit

Companies with Limited Liability

These companies are controlled by the terms of the Civil Code generally, although in practice many of the bases underlying the presentation and format of their financial statements are outlined by the internal revenue code (testo unico della Leggi sulle Imposte Dirette). Limited companies are comprised of:

1 Public companies (Società Per Azioni – SPA) which must have: at least two members; a definite (though extendable) life span; a minimum capital of one million lire (£670); freely transferable shares; and no rights to purchase their own shares except where shareholders specifically approve purchase of fully paid up shares out of profits. Audited annual accounts must be filed with the Registrar of Enterprises, but there is no legal requirement for the directors' report to be examined and reported upon.
2 Private companies (Società a Responsabilita Limitata – SRL) which have a minimum capital of 50000 lire (£33) and restricted right of transfer of interest. Shares are not normally issued, interests being represented by quotas of at least 1000 lire (£0.7), and debentures are not allowed. In other respects – accounts, directors, minimum members – the requirements are similar to those of an SPA.

Cooperatives

Cooperatives may be formed for production, marketing, banking and insurance activities, each participant being restricted to a maximum quota of shares of approximately £150. These cooperatives may be:

1   Società Cooperativa a Responsabilita Limitata – SCRL – with limited liability.
2   Società Cooperativa a Responsabilita Illimitata – SCRIL – with unlimited liability.

Partnerships

Partnerships, all classed as separate entities for tax purposes, may be:

1   General (Società in Nome Collettivo – SNC), the normal commercial form.
2   Limited (Società in Accomandita Semplice – SAS), with at least one general partner.
3   Limited with shares (Società in Accomandita Per Azioni – SAPA) where shareholders have transferable shares and limited liability but where there must be at least one general partner (director). This form of partnership has a separate legal entity.

Fiduciang and auditing companies

Società Fiduciarie e di Revisione (Fiduciary and auditing companies) may be either companies or partnerships formed for property administration, consultancy or shareholder representation purposes. They cannot undertake any work specifically requiring a personal involvement – corporation audit, trusteeship – and must file annual accounts with the Ministry of Industry and Commerce.

Sole Traders with Unlimited Liability

Branches of Foreign Enterprises

A branch of a foreign enterprise is not recognized as a separate legal entity and its liabilities are those of its parent company. It must file annual accounts, and particulars of its authorization and personal representatives.

Business Records

As in France, the Civil Code requires the use of a journal and inventory book, prenumbered and stamped by a notary public or the Court. Companies must also maintain minute books and a share register and, in satisfaction of the tax and labour laws, certain other books, and records such as payroll and personnel, records of fixed assets, payments to third parties, chart of accounts etc.

The Accounting Profession

The accounting profession in Italy is largely regulated under the Ministry of Justice which has stipulated the rules, conduct, fees and duties of the profession. The profession is also influenced to some extent by the Civil Code as regards the auditing function.

Rather than being organized at national level, the profession tends to be administered regionally, with locally elected national representatives. There are two types of professional accountant, both governed by laws passed in 1953: Doctors of Commerce, and Accountants and Commercial Experts. The Doctors of Commerce (Ordine dei Dottori Commercialisti) represent the academic wing of the Italian profession. Qualification is by means of a four-year university course in economics; accounting; banking; public, civil and commercial law. The requirements also include a doctoral thesis, followed by a state examination in accounting and company law. There is no requirement for practical experience and a Dottori Commercialista does not have to practise to retain the title.

The Accountants and Commercial Experts (Collegio dei Ragionieri e Periti Commerciali) are qualified to a greater extent by practice and experience. Membership of the Collegio is obtained by means of passing the accounting diploma examinations in accounting, mathematics, business law and economics – usually taken during a five-year technical college course. At least two year's practical experience must be obtained with a member of the Collegio or the Ordine in public practice, and a state examination must be passed in the provisions of the Civil Code, accounting, company law and taxation. The work which members of either the Collegio or the Ordine are empowered to undertake is identical and both are held competent to carry out the statutory audits of companies, subject to their being on the official professional lists. This entry is limited to qualified persons of Italian nationality, who have gained admittance to a local ordine or collegio organization, as appropriate. Any company must have a Board of Auditors (Collegio Sindacale) who are appointed to carry out the statutory audit. In the case of a company with a share capital of less than 50 million lire the board is comprised of three or five auditors (Sindaci) and two alternates (substitutes who take the place of Sindaci if, for some reason, the latter are unable to act). At least one of the auditors and one of the alternates must be chosen from the official list of professionals (albi professionali). In the case of companies with a share capital of 50 million lire (£33 000) or above, the chairman of the board plus one alternate member – plus, if there are five board members, one other auditor – must be chosen from the official list of auditors (ruolo dei revisori ufficiali dei conti). Membership of this list is restricted to Italian nationals who have served at least five years as an active statutory auditor or as a director, administrative or accounting officer of a limited company with capital not less than 50 million lire or who have satisfactorily performed other duties. Thus the position of statutory auditor, while open to members of the Ordine and the Collegio, is not their exclusive prerogative but is also open to people who do not necessarily possess any accounting skill or experience.

Practising Dottori or Ragioniéri usually do so as sole practitioners, but the partnership practice form is forbidden. Currently there are 15 000 Dottori, of whom it is estimated that 8000 are in practice, and 7000 Ragionieri of whom 6000 are deemed to be in practice; their work includes 140 quoted companies with a total market capitalization of £4000 million, although this ignores the numerous small businesses which exist under both the SPA and SRL types of organization. The type of work undertaken by the profession, as well as auditing, includes special investigations, business and tax consultancy, liquidations, receiverships, estate administration and arbitration. Attempts are being made to amalgamate the two accounting bodies but as yet this has not been done.

While there is no code of ethics drawn up, there are certain legal principles which govern professional behaviour. No practising accountant of either body can carry on a second business outside his professional activities. Fees for statutory audits are fixed by the Ministry of Justice and are based on company characteristics such as share capital or total assets, or income. The holding of shares in a company is not deemed incompatible with holding an appointment as one of the board of auditors, although some relationships (such as director or other contractual employment) are banned. Rules governing professionals and their relationship with clients and others have been stipulated by the Ministry of Justice.

Statutory Requirements

The company in Italy, in common with partnerships, is governed by the regulations contained in the Italian Civil Code, as supplemented by the fiscal regulations and the company's own Memorandum of Association. An interesting facet of the Italian company scene is that many of the public limited companies are very small in size, corresponding more to the image of the small private company. This situation has largely been brought about by the effect of inflation on the minimum capital requirement for an SPA, which no longer restricts such an organizational structure to the larger concern. Current statutory requirements covering limited companies are included in the overall practices summarized in the summary below.

Standards

Auditing

Professional audit standards are virtually nonexistent since there is no national auditing body to propose or recommend them. Italian auditors tend to restrict their duties within the legal requirements imposed on them by the Civil Code. This requires them to keep check on the company's management. Specifically, they must meet at least quarterly to examine the company's cash and securities, review the financial statements and check them to the inventory ledger and review the values assigned to assets as laid down in the Code. It is understood that an act reforming company law is under review, although there seems to be little improvement contemplated in the standard of auditing required.

Reporting

No standard form of auditor's report exists, the usual form merely stating that:

1   The particular examinations required by the law have been carried out and found to be satisfactory.
2   Asset values are in accordance with the legal rules.
3   The financial accounts are therefore recommended to the shareholders. It must also be remembered that the law includes the requirements of the internal revenue code which may from time to time contradict, as well as support, the requirements of the Civil Code.

There are no provisions for the presentation of a report of management.

Accounting

There are no recommendations on accounting principles. Those standards in use are decreed by the Civil Code, which prescribes the content but not the form of the final accounts, and specifies the principles of valuation to be applied to certain assets and liabilities. In practice, the Code is overridden by the requirements of the tax regulations as to the showing of allowable items, plus the need to preserve a 'bargaining' position in order to minimize liability. There is some hope that the contemplated reform act for companies may regularize, if not raise, the standards to be used in providing accounting information. The more significant practices encountered in Italy are included in the summary.

Extra-statutory Requirements

The Italian capital markets are still rudimentary by international standards, the majority of firms never thinking to raise risk capital through stock markets, and thus the Stock Exchanges play only a marginal role in the provision of capital for industry and seem likely to do so for some time to come. Much of this capital is provided by means of internal financing or bank loan, and there is a plethora of regional and sectional financing and concessionary credit schemes subject to statutory regulation. Too often they are inadequate in scope. Other factors inhibiting the development of an active capital market are:

1 Political instability, which tends to delay the implementation of reforms.
2 The particular method of taxation administration, which instils a predilection for minimum disclosure of information together with an avoidance of any form of formally registered investment such as shares.

Since bearer shares are generally prohibited by Italian law, the would-be equity investor is prevented, in effect, from investing. Those share dealings which do take place are largely handled by the banks and not the Stock Exchanges, and the narrowness both of the listings themselves and the holders of shares tends to allow considerable potential for manipulation of share prices by a few institutions, and/or private investors. There are, therefore, no extra-statutory requirements, reliance being placed solely on legislation.

Professional Bodies

There are no extra-statutory requirements set by the professional bodies, largely because of the abundance of legal requirements, and also because of the organization of the professional bodies on a regional rather than a national basis. Thus, while some regional bodies have an informal code of ethics, there are none formulated on a national basis. Nor are there any national auditing or accounting standards.

Stock Exchange

Italian Stock Exchanges are state-controlled and run in the style of public service industries. Consequently, they operate within a seemingly rigid framework which precludes any apparent need for extra-statutory controls. In fact, there would seem to be a considerable need for such controls because of:

1 The narrowness and other imperfections of the market.
2 The lack of a compensation fund for the protection of investors.
3 Broker competition.
4 The amount of dealing carried on outside the market.

Financial reporting requirements There are no requirements imposed by the Stock Exchange concerning financial reporting, other than the provision of annual accounts as approved by the shareholders. Thus, the standard of reporting depends almost entirely on the company involved and there is, understandably, a wide variation in quality. The minimum standard of reporting is governed by the Civil Code.

Listing requirements and prospectuses There are no extra-statutory requirements concerning quotations. These are governed by a mixture of the Civil Code and statutory requirements of the Treasury Department as administered by the local Chamber of Commerce. A prospectus must be issued outlining the purpose of the issue and status of shares, and containing a statement that the requirements of the Civil Code have been met. In addition, there must be evidence:

1 Of the shareholders' approval of the last two years' accounts.
2 That profits have been made.
3 That no dividends or interest are in arrears.

Some exchanges impose a minimum capital requirement before listing.

Takeover and Merger Requirements
There is no system of extra-statutory control regarding takeovers and mergers since most of these operations are subject to government intervention. This intervention is largely a result of attempts both to promote regional policies and to obviate the outflow of capital from Italy. Most takeover operations are the subject of private deals and agreements, often backed by the government-promoted statutory bodies.

Summary of the Principal Areas of Current Accounting and Reporting Requirements in Italy

Accountant's Report to be Included in a Prospectus for the Sale of Securities

Although a prospectus must be issued outlining the purpose of the issue, there is no requirement for an independent accountant's report. The status of the shares must be stated and a declaration made that the requirements of the Civil Code have been met. The financial accounts for the last two years must be presented. Evidence must be presented that:

1   The shareholders have approved the last two years' accounts.
2   The last two years have resulted in profits.
3   No dividends or interest are in arrear.

Form and Content of Published Accounts

All limited companies, public and private, are required to file copies of their audited annual balance sheet and profit and loss account with the local Registrar of Enterprises and publish them in the official gazette. The directors' report is also subject to filing and publication requirements. Auditors must carry out a cash and securities check and examine the financial statements to date at least once every three months. No fixed form is prescribed for the balance sheet. The Civil Code specifies headings, but does not outline any particular grouping or format. Fixed assets, inventories and current assets must all be separately headed. A legal reserve has to be maintained and separated from the termination indemnity reserves which the Civil Code now requires to be built up. Liabilities must distinguish secured from unsecured items although no further details are required.

There are no requirements concerning the profit and loss account, other than that it must be included as part of the published financial statements. Consequently, it is usually prepared in an exceedingly condensed form. Supportive information, if provided at all, is often restricted to a few memorandum accounts. There are no requirements for the presentation of consolidated accounts and they are therefore not normally prepared. For the same reason, relevant information on holdings and affiliations is not provided in any generalized manner. Some of the larger firms do publish some operating statistics on their unconsolidated subsidiaries and a number of firms have utilized the equity method in accounting for investments in subsidiaries.

There is no standard form of audit report, the usual form merely certifying that the statutory examinations have been carried out and found to be satisfactory, that asset values are in accordance with the legal rules, and the accounts are therefore recommended to the shareholders.

There is no statutory requirement for a management report, although if presented, the directors' report would give details of any departure from the valuation principles stipulated by the Civil Code. It would also state any material events which, occurring after the balance sheet date, affect the financial position or reported income. Distributions and appropriations of profit, subject to the requirements concerning the legal reserve, are to be authorized by the shareholders in general meeting.

Current Practice

Fixed assets The basis of fixed asset value is cost, although a general revaluation was permitted in 1952, and specific revaluations may be permitted if there are special reasons for this. Extraordinary repairs and initial financing costs may be capitalized and depreciated, and conversely, capital items may be charged to revenue if there are likely tax advantages. Depreciation is normally charged according to the rules of tax legislation which permits straight-line calculation only, at prescribed rates according to industry and asset type. The rules also prescribe accelerated charges which are normally charged in the financial accounts, in order to be claimable, although in poor years the firm might not charge depreciation because of the lack of any direct tax advantage. Such changes in practice are unlikely to be disclosed. Figures are shown at cost with the depreciation (termed amortization) reserves shown on the liabilities side of the balance sheet.

Goodwill and intangibles Intangibles tend to be carried forward and amortized according to the prescriptive tax rules. Goodwill can only be recorded when it results from a purchase and must be written off within a reasonable time as judged by the directors and auditors.

Investments There is no distinction between long- and short-term holdings although marketable securities are separated from investments in subsidiaries and associates. Valuation is based on the lower of cost or market value and it is not normal practice to disclose a market value, even with quoted securities. The emphasis is towards under rather than over statement, and where an investment has been written down it may be retained at that figure even if the market value subsequently increases.

Current assets and stocks These are valued at the lower of cost or market value. Stocks are valued on an item by item basis in applying the cost or market rule. Cost includes overhead, and market price is defined as replacement cost. In practice, it is usual to assume a FIFO flow or use a moving average for purposes of arriving at cost both for financial and tax purposes. However, it is unlikely that the method used would be disclosed. Since no lower valuation limit is set by Italian law, it is not unusual for stocks to be undervalued. Debtors are to be shown at estimated realizable value, but, since tax law does not allow relief for bad debts until evidence can be produced as to their uncollectability, it is unusual to find provisions for general doubtful debts. Any such provisions would be shown as a reserve on the liabilities side of the balance sheet. There is no legal distinction between current and fixed assets.

Deferred charges In the case of discount on debentures, these must be written off as prescribed by the Civil Code. Preliminary expenses must be written off within five years.

Liabilities Differentiation is made between long- and short-term liabilities but, apart from this, very little extra information as to interest rates, due dates, security lodged, is given. Debentures are usually restricted in total amount to the amount of paid up capital.

Reserves and provisions A legal reserve is required to be maintained of at least 20% of the share capital issued and, until it reaches this proportion, 5% of net profits must be appropriated annually. Share premiums and profits from sales of own repurchased shares may be used for this purpose but the legal reserve may only be used to absorb losses, except for any portion of the reserve above the required 20%. A company's articles may require particular reserves known as extraordinary reserves. Those monetary revaluation reserves which still exist following the 1952 revaluations can now be used as the shareholders and directors decide. Taxed reserve is the name given to the account to which retrospective adjustments are made for finally settled discrepancies between the financial and tax rules, eg capitalized, disallowed repairs or depreciation excessively written off, etc (see 'Income statement' below). Other reserves are listed in specific detail. Secret reserves are common, arising from excessive depreciation, write-down of securities and investments and an overprovision for contingencies. However, this may well be offset by an imprudent provision for the tax liability (see 'Income statement' below). It is not normal practice, nor required by law, to show movements on reserves.

Share capital All shares must have a par value, may not be in the form of bearer shares (except on certain geographical grounds) and may be repurchased by the company. Own shares which have been repurchased must be shown separately in the assets. Shareholders equity is not subtotalled and profit/loss is separated from the capital section. Where accumulated losses amount to more than one third of capital the shareholders are required to reduce the capital or contribute new capital to redress the proportion unless the subsequent year's profits provide such redress. Where the net assets fall below the minimum for the particular type of organization, the company must either change its constitution or net assets must be increased in conjunction with a reduction of capital. Bonus issues are made at par and dividends (proposed) are part of the distributable profits shown in the balance sheet.

Accounting for acquisitions and mergers The pooling of interests method has been used by a few firms although there is little commonality of method applied to accounting for acquisitions and mergers.

Income statement There are no legal classification requirements at all for the profit and loss account which, consequently, is normally presented in a very condensed form, although the proposed reform act for companies does include some detailed classification. Neither sales nor cost of sales is usually disclosed and the profit and loss account normally commences with gross profit. Depreciation for the year is usually shown as a separate item although, as stated under 'Fixed assets', it is not necessarily calculated on a consistent basis, may well be excessive, and will most certainly be governed more by tax motives than financial or reporting ones. The basis of the provision will not be disclosed, nor is the amount of wages and salaries likely to be disclosed. Charges and investment income are usually shown but not in sufficient detail to allow much differentiation between alternative sources. Prior-year and extraordinary items or adjustments are seldom distinguished from current, ordinary expenses and revenues.

Taxation accounting, in the sense that the tax rules decree a common basis for financial and tax accounts, is practised in Italy. This has the expected result of distorting financial statements towards minimizing revenues and maximizing expenses, and produces a reluctance to defer charges beyond any year in which either profit is low or losses have been sustained. However, the strong pressure towards profit minimization often produces the opposite effect to that intended because of the peculiar method of assessing liability on a firm. In certain specified cases which are in practice, fairly general, tax is assessed by the 'inductive' method of estimating a liability, the final assessment being the result of a process of bargaining between the assessor and the firm. Understandably, in order to preserve the strength of its bargaining position, a firm tends to keep profits as recorded to a minimum but at the same time, because the whole process is likely to take some considerable time and in order not to acknowledge a likely outcome of the negotiations, the tax charge in the accounts is restricted to amounts actually paid. Thus the recorded figure for tax would be well below the tax liability based upon profits. The outcome of the negotiations is also likely to involve adjustments through the 'taxed reserve' (see 'Reserves and provisions' above) for disallowed items etc, relating to earlier years.

Thus, far from having a deferred system of accounting for taxation many firms do not even systematically accrue for it. Although tax legislation for reform is under consideration, it is not proposed to alter the method of assessment.

Appropriations are not normally differentiated, and any directors' bonus would normally be charged to distributable profits as shown in the balance sheet.

Other points Accounting policies used in preparing the accounts are not disclosed and from the point of view of UK accounting may apply only the one concept of going-concern. As outlined above, even the policy of conservatism is not fully carried out because of the failure to accrue the likely tax liability. Notes to the accounts are unlikely to appear, although certain items such as contingencies may be shown in memorandum accounts below the balance sheet totals. The effects of changes in accounting methods are unlikely to be disclosed, as are the changes themselves. Similarly, there is unlikely to be any indication of capital commitments, although material post-dated events are often disclosed in the directors' report.

Current Trends

Statutory Trends

There are three kinds of statutory trend in Italy at present: the reform of stock market rules, company law reform and tax law reform.

Reform of stock market rules In April 1974 a supervisory commission was established to control quoted companies and Stock Exchange activities. It is modelled to some extent on the US Securities and Exchange Commission and its purposes are to stem the flow of capital abroad and encourage the raising of company finance by means of risk capital rather than bank borrowing. Most of the points in the 12-article decree can be seen as attempts to increase stock market activity and stabilize quoted prices. Currently, only about 150 firms are quoted. The articles include:

1   Authorising the commission to regulate dealing, listing and quotation practices on the Stock Exchange.
2   Authorising the commission to stipulate the form and content of quoted company balance sheets, and to appoint inspectors to supervise the accuracy of reported information.
3   The prohibition of cross shareholdings in excess of 3% of a quoted company's share capital.
4   The introduction of the right for shareholders to elect to incur a 'flat-rate' 30% dividend tax leaving the remaining 70% tax-free.

In addition, it is proposed that banks' dealings should be channelled through the Exchange, that the number of provincial Exchanges should be reduced, and that brokers should be allowed to form partnerships.

Company law reform Proposals for company law reform were published in October 1973 but have not yet been adopted. The draft proposals improve considerably the quality of information required of published financial statements, particularly that concerned with the profitability of an enterprise. The proposals include the following:

1   That a register of accounting firms authorized to conduct quoted company audits should be established. This register will be compiled by the supervisory commission. It is likely that initially the only firms capable of meeting the standards required for registration will be the larger international firms, including the Swiss fiduciary and auditing firms, currently operating in Italy.
2   The acceptance, for tax purposes, of the balance sheet of a company where that balance sheet is attested by such a registered audit firm.
3   The inclusion in the published financial statements of a quoted company, of both a detailed profit and loss account and information on associated company shareholdings.
4   The introduction of special savings shares, carrying no voting rights but receiving higher dividend rates and taxed somewhat less heavily than ordinary shares.

The proposals do not, however, provide for the separation of operational income from other income, disclosure of valuation methods or the presentation of a detailed report of management.

Tax law reform Studies on the reform of direct taxation are proceeding. Apart from the dispensation to certain quoted companies described in point 2 under 'Company law reform', the proposals in their current form will do nothing to alter the system of tax assessment. It seems, therefore, that there will be little general improvement in financial reporting practice resulting from this reform, as the incentive to retain a favourable bargaining position will remain.

Other Trends

The attempts to widen the reliance of business on the private provision of risk capital must be seen in the current climate of the Italian economy. This is dominated by a few state-owned holding companies and most long-term finance is raised through Government-controlled institutions. These institutions already hold between 28–43% of the shares in most major companies. Furthermore, it has been estimated that equity shareholdings account for only 20–30% of company finance in Italian industry, and that 85% of all new issues are fixed interest securities. In such a situation, the attempts to widen the basis of stock market activity are likely to be, at best, difficult to achieve.

The Italian system of accounting does not appear to be sufficiently developed to fit within any one of the four patterns identified by Mueller and described in chapter 1. However, to the extent that the legal framework within which it is confined is largely influenced by fiscal policy considerations, and because of the leading role played by Government-promoted institutions, it is likely that any development of the system of accounting will adopt a macroeconomic orientation.

11

Luxembourg

Type of Business Unit

Companies with Limited Liability

These companies are controlled by the Luxembourg Commercial Code as supplemented by the law on commercial companies. Within this classification are:

1 Public companies (Société Anonyme – SA), which have similar requirements to the Belgian SAs as regards number of shareholders, transferability of shares, limited life and directors. Audited annual accounts must be filed and published together with the statutory auditors' (commissaires') and directors' reports.
2 Private companies (Société de Personnes à Responsabilité Limitée – SPRL) are again based on the Belgian pattern as to membership life and restrictions on both transferability and size of shareholdings. The form of SPRL is not permitted in insurance and banking businesses.

Cooperatives

Cooperatives may be:

1 Société Cooperative with Association Momentanée (AM).
2 Société Cooperative with Association Commerciale en Participation (A CEN P).

Both types must register and file accounts with the local commercial registrar.

Partnerships

Partnerships may be:

1   General (Société en Nom Collectif – SEN NC) with joint and several liability.
2   Limited (Société en Commandite Simple – SEN CS) with at least one general partner. Annual accounts must be filed.
3   Limited with shares (Société en Commandite par Actions – SCA) with limited, transferable shareholder liability and at least one general partner. Such an organization is subject to statutory audit, and accounts must be published.

Sole Traders with Unlimited Liability

Branches of Foreign Corporations

A branch of a foreign corporation may be established, but is not recognized as a separate legal entity. The publication and filing requirements for foreign, quoted companies are the same as those for domestic quoted companies. Nonresident investment is subject to government approval.

Business Records

The Commercial Code requires the keeping of officially stamped and prenumbered journal and book of balances, and a share register. Again, on the Belgian model, official sales, purchases and personnel records are required as a result of tax and labour laws.

The Accounting Profession

The accounting profession in Luxembourg is principally carried on by L'Ordre des Experts Comptables Luxembourgeois, which has a current membership of 24. Members, who must be Luxembourg nationals, qualify by becoming graduates and completing a three-year period of articles under a member of L'Ordre. In the case of a business graduate the period of articles may be reduced to 18 months. The service under articles may include a maximum of one year in the service of an approved public accountant outside Luxembourg and a further maximum of one year in industry. In any event, the minimum age at which a student can be admitted to membership is 24 years. Unlike in Belgium, the professional Expert Comptable in Luxembourg must be in practice. If, after admittance to L'Ordre, he ceases to be in practice and undertakes employment in industry or commerce, he must renounce membership of L'Ordre. The type of work undertaken by the Expert Comptable typically includes audit and accounting work generally, tax and business consultancy, formation and liquidation work, investigations for management, and corporate planning. A member of L'Ordre practises as a sole practitioner or in partnership. L'Ordre has a Code of Ethics specifically concerned with members' independence, and with relationships among themselves and with clients.

All partnerships limited by shares, and limited companies, must undergo an annual statutory audit. However, the persons entitled to carry out the audit are not specified by law and therefore it is not necessarily the prerogative of the Expert Comptable. Indeed, lawyers, employees or relatives may carry out the function of the statutory examiner (commissaire). Their duties are to inspect relevant books and documents, and to report to the shareholders as to the accuracy of the accounts. There are current moves to restrict such statutory work to the Expert Comptable.

Statutory Requirements

The position in Luxembourg as regards company legislation is similar to that in Belgium. The main provisions are contained in a somewhat outdated Commercial Code, and the more detailed aspects of the requirements are found in tax legislation. These requirements are included in the summary below.

Standards

Auditing

There are no recommended auditing standards and the methods in use are an amalgam of the requirements of the Commercial Code, the law on commercial companies and the tax laws. As in Belgium, the statutory auditors are required to observe and, if necessary, to call the attention of the shareholders to, the acts of the management, and also to report on the accounts, stating the verification of cash and securities. The fiscal laws require all allowable items to be shown on the face of the published or filed accounts, and such laws have tended to prescribe the valuation principles in use.

Reporting

There is no standard form of auditor's report, although both a statutory short-form, and a long-form report to the management are usually presented. The short-form report certifies that the legal requirements have been met. The directors must report to the shareholders, and to the supervisory board if there is one, outlining details of partly paid up share capital and showing the proposed profit appropriations.

Accounting

There are no recommendations on accounting principles, standards being derived from the Commercial Code and company and fiscal legislation. There is no specified form of financial statement other than that prescribed for banks and certain insurance companies. Current requirements are included in the summary below.

Extra-statutory Requirements

The financial scene in Luxembourg is similar to that in Belgium and there has been little pressure for the introduction of extra-statutory requirements.

Professional Bodies

There are no statements or recommendations issued by the professional bodies either in the form of controls or even for members' guidance.

Stock Exchange

Investment is largely handled by the banks or by the state institutions. The Commissaire au Controle des Banques exercises a supervisory role with regard to stock exchange listings.

    Financial reporting requirements There are no formal requirements concerning published financial information other than that contained in company legislation.

    Listing requirements and prospectuses The Commissaire au Controle des Banques must give approval before permission can be obtained for a stock exchange listing. Requirements are included in the summary.

Takeover and Merger Requirements

There is no established code covering takeover and merger practices.

Summary of the Principal Areas of Current Accounting and Reporting Requirements in Luxembourg

Accountant's Report to be Included in a Prospectus for the Sale of Securities

There is no requirement for an independent accountant's report or a profit forecast. However, considerable detail as to the purpose of the issue, details of underwriting arrangements and particulars of shares held by interested parties are required by the Banking Commission. In addition, the Commission requires a schedule of liabilities and contingent liabilities, and can investigate the accuracy of the information presented to it. The Stock Exchange requires the previous two years' balance sheets to be published and the Commercial Code requires details of the Company's objects, capital structure, unpaid capital, directors, and assets to be purchased out of the proceeds of the issue.

Form and Content of Published Accounts

All limited companies are required to file an audited copy of the financial accounts at the local commercial court. These accounts must be audited and consist of the balance sheet and profit and loss account, profit appropriation statement, an analysis of share capital, together with details of any holders of unpaid capital and a list of directors and auditors. There is no requirement to file a copy of the auditor's report. The profit appropriation must be in accordance with the shareholders' authorization. The financial accounts must also be published in the official gazette.

There is no fixed format for a balance sheet (other than for banks and certain insurance companies) but there must be shown separately: fixed assets, current assets, capital, reserves and surplus, shareholders' equity, secured and unsecured debentures and other liabilities. A legal reserve must be maintained but no valuation principles are outlined. There are no requirements concerning the profit and loss account other than that 'appropriate' depreciation shall be charged. Consequently, the profit and loss account is normally presented in an abridged form.

There are no requirements for the presentation of consolidated accounts and such accounts are specifically precluded from being substituted for the balance sheets of investment companies and investment funds. Consequently, the presentation of consolidated statements is hardly ever practised. Investments in subsidiaries are shown at cost, less any (undisclosed) contingency reserves. Accounting for subsidiaries on an equity basis is rarely practised.

There is no standard form of auditors' report. Usually two reports are presented:

1 A short-form certificate dealing with compliance with the law and the verification of cash and securities.
2 A long-form report, including the certificate, which is made to the management and would require them to bring any irregular acts of management to the attention of the shareholders. It also explains and supplements certain of the balances in the financial accounts.

The directors must report to the shareholders and the supervisory board, if one is in existence. Such a report would include a statement showing the proposed profit allocation and details of any partly paid up share capital, including the names and addresses of such partly paid up shareholders.

Current Practice

Fixed assets Fixed assets are basically valued at cost, and generally subject to the limitations imposed in other European countries where the financial accounts are prepared on a common basis with taxation regulations. Depreciation is allowed on the reducing balance method for tax purposes on all fixed assets other than buildings, on which depreciation is not allowed, and therefore tends not to be charged in the financial accounts. In the case of fixed assets with a value not exceeding L Fr 15 000 (£150) they can be written off in the year of acquisition. The facilities for providing excessive depreciation or deferring depreciation are in line with the other tax-accounting systems.

Goodwill and intangibles These are generally shown at cost, but are written off either over the life of a relevant asset or over a short period. Goodwill may be allowed, as it is amortized, for tax purposes according to specific rules.

Investments There is seldom any differentiation made between investments in affiliates, subsidiaries or others and they are valued according to cost or market rules. It is unlikely that market values are disclosed, even in the case of quoted investments. However, a list of investments is usually given.

Current assets and stocks These are valued on the cost or market basis, but with provisions against debtors only recognized for tax purposes when the debt becomes irrecoverable. Stocks are likely to be valued, in practice for tax purposes, on an individual item basis, cost to include overheads, and by an average, specific or FIFO method. LIFO and base stock methods are not permitted for tax purposes and therefore not used in financial accounts. It is unlikely that the basis of stock pricing would be disclosed. The tax rules permit certain commodity stocks to be reduced to the lowest prices ruling on world markets within the last five years and it is not uncommon for stocks generally to be written down in order to smooth income between periods. No disclosure of such practices is likely. Distinction is made between immovable and realizable assets.

Deferred charges Preliminary expenses are amortized over a relatively short period and, if in accordance with tax rules, such amortization will be allowed.

Liabilities Differentiation tends to be between long- and short-term although secured liabilities would also be distinguished. There is little disclosure of interest rates or duration other than the one-year dividing line implied between long- and short-term.

Reserves and provisions A legal reserve is required to be maintained of at least 10% of the share capital and, until it reaches this proportion, 5% of profits must be appropriated annually. Such a reserve may only be used to absorb losses, or, if in excess of 10%, it may be capitalized. Restricted reserves are nondistributable and often stipulated by the company's articles. Free reserves are the appropriations of profits authorized by the shareholders for distribution. Any premiums on shares may be added to such free reserves, or capitalized according to the shareholders' wishes. Any surplus remaining from the revaluation of property or other fixed assets would appear in a specific reserve. Secret reserves are common, arising from excessive depreciation, stock and investment writedowns and over-provision for contingencies. It is not normal practice to show movements on reserves.

Share capital Shares must have a par value. They may be in the form of bearer shares, but they cannot be repurchased by the company. Share capital must be fully subscribed and, in the case of bearer shares, fully paid up before issue. In the case of registered shares, issue may be made when 20% of the price is paid, unless the price is in kind, in which case the share must be fully paid up on issue. Bonus issues are generally made at par and dividends are part of the distributed profit figure shown on the balance sheet, proposed dividends normally not being provided.

Accounting for acquisitions and mergers There is little standardization of practice other than the lack of use of the pooling of interests method.

Income statement There are no legal classification requirements for the profit and loss account which, accordingly, is normally presented in a very abridged form. Neither sales nor cost of sales is normally disclosed and the account normally commences with gross profit. Depreciation for the year is usually shown as a separate item and, because of the tax requirements for items claimed to be charged in the financial accounts, will be taxation orientated rather than financially orientated. The basis of the provision is unlikely to be disclosed. Wages and salaries are unlikely to be shown, although financial and debt charges and investment and financial income are likely to be shown in the aggregate. Prior-year or extraordinary items are seldom distinguished. Taxation accounting is normal practice, but there is no deferred system of accounting for differences between estimates and actual liabilities. Appropriations are not normally included in the statement, although an analysis of the allocation and approved distributions are normally published. Payments to directors for fees, salaries etc, are normally regarded as appropriations.

Other points As mentioned earlier, financial statements may only serve to show the 'minimum position' and as such the overriding concepts are those of conservatism and the tax rules. Supplementary notes are unusual although memorandum accounts with regard to contingencies are sometimes given. Changes in accounting methods, post-date events or capital commitments are unlikely to be disclosed and comparative figures are only required for quoted companies.

Current Trends

Probably the most important trend is the attempt to restrict statutory auditing to the Expert Comptable. If the attempt succeeds, it will no doubt eventually pave the way to the establishing of standards in reporting and disclosure practices. The Commissaire au Controle des Banques has evolved a specific format for the financial statements to be issued by banks and certain insurance companies, and this may eventually influence the statements of industrial concerns.

The accounting system in Luxembourg, with its dependence on the taxation legislation, implies a macroeconomic orientation within the context of Mueller's identified patterns described in Chapter 1.

12

Sweden

Type of Business Unit

Companies with Limited Liability

There is only one type of limited liability company currently recognized under Swedish law. That is the Aktiebolag – AB. Despite the proposals contained in the Nordic Companies Act (a harmonization of the company law of Denmark, Finland, Norway and Sweden) no differentiation is made in Sweden between public and private limited companies. The rules are applied according to whether an AB is above a certain size and/or whether it has obtained a quotation.

An AB must have at least three founders who must be resident Swedish citizens or entities, but after incorporation membership may fall as low as one person. There is a minimum share capital requirement of S Kr 5000 (£500) or, where the company's statute states a maximum share capital, one-third of any such maximum provided that such a figure is greater than S Kr 5000. There is a minimum share value of S Kr 10 (£1) for companies whose share capital does not exceed S Kr 50000 (£5000); otherwise, the minimum value is S Kr 50 (£5). Under the Nordic proposals these minima for par values would be dispensed with, although 'no-par-value' shares would not be allowed. Shares must be 50% paid up before registration, the balance being due within two years. Shares, in almost all cases, must be registered, and are freely transferable. Annual accounts, consisting of the balance sheet, profit and loss account and directors' report, must be audited and filed.

In any company whose share capital, issued or authorized, exceeds S Kr 500000 (£50000) there must be at least three directors and a managing director who need not be one of the three. Such a company must also have at least two auditors. Where a company is quoted, or where its share capital exceeds S Kr 2 million (£200000), at least one of the auditors must be an authorized public accountant. Quite frequently state enterprise is carried on in the form of a joint stock company.

Cooperatives

Cooperatives (Ekonomisk Forening) are an important form of agricultural and/or consumer organization, although they are governed by a separate Cooperative Societies Act.

Partnerships

Partnerships may be:

1 General (Handelsbolag) which is the commercial form of unlimited partnership involving joint and several liability.
2 Limited (Kommanditbolag) which must have at least one general (unlimited) partner. General partners are jointly and severally liable for the firm's debts, the limited partners only being liable to the extent of their contributed capital.
3 Civil (Enkeltbolag) a noncommercial form of general partnership which need not be registered in the commercial register.

To date partnerships have not been a particularly popular form of organization, largely because of the relatively low minimum capital requirements needed for incorporation as a limited company.

Sole Traders with Unlimited Liability

Branches of Foreign Companies

A branch of a foreign company may be established in Sweden subject to Government permission. This is normally granted, except in certain specified activities, provided that the application is made by a parent company which is also operating within its own country of origin. In general terms, the branch is subject to the same rules as those companies resident and domiciled in Sweden. It must, however, keep a separate set of books, appoint a Swedish resident (although not necessarily a national) as manager, and appoint a Swedish authorized public accountant as auditor. The manager's report, audit report, and annual accounts, must be filed with the Registrar of Companies where there is a requirement for publication in the home country of the branch head office. In any event, the above documents must be filed with the Royal Patent and Registration Office where any person can inspect them. Tax liability is normally similar to that of a Swedish company. The manager must possess an unlimited power of attorney and the name of the branch must include the name of the owner company, its country of incorporation, and the word 'filial'.

Business Records

Business records generally are governed by the Bookkeeping Law 1929. This specifically requires the keeping of a journal for daily transactions and an inventory book for the annual recording of assets and liabilities. Both books must be bound and the pages pre-numbered. In addition, the law requires the keeping of such other records as are necessary, considering the size and activities of the organization, in accordance with generally accepted bookkeeping practices. This law is currently under revision. The Companies Act of 1944 specifically requires a limited company to keep a share register. It also stipulates the form and content of the annual financial statements.

The Accounting Profession

The accounting profession in Sweden is mainly carried on by the Auktoriserad Revisor (AR) – authorized public accountant – although a junior qualification also exists, that of Godkander Granskningsman (GG) – approved examiner of accounts. The AR obtains his authorization from the Swedish chambers of commerce, of which there are twelve, and the earliest authorization was granted in 1912 by the Stockholm Chamber of Commerce. A candidate for authorization must possess a degree in economics (or its equivalent) from a Swedish school of economics. The course is a full-time one of at least three years and must include specialization in economics, business administration (with special emphasis on accounting and auditing) and law (with special emphasis on business law). Passes in business administration and law are required at honours grades. There is provision for a candidate other than an economics undergraduate, to sit an examination in similar subjects, set by staff of the schools of economics, in lieu of the degree examinations. However, to date less than 5% of ARs have qualified by this alternative method. After obtaining his academic qualification, the candidate must spend at least five years in the employment of a practising AR on relevant work. On completion of this period of training and experience he may apply for authorization to his relevant chamber of commerce. He must also satisfy the chamber that he is a Swedish citizen, is at least 25 years old and is a 'free agent'. In order to ensure comparable standards between the chambers of commerce, a coordinating Central Accountants' Board of the Chambers of Commerce must approve the application before authorization is granted. The AR therefore qualifies by a mixture of academic examination and professional experience, but does not undergo any professional examination.

ARs are organized nationally through the Association of Authorized Public Accountants (Foreningen Aukteriserade Revisorer – FAR). The FAR dates from 1923 and an AR can apply for membership provided: he has been authorized as a public accountant by a chamber of commerce; that he has been in practice as such for at least one year immediately preceding his application to join the FAR; that he intends to continue in practice; and he is judged to be suitable and possess sufficient integrity. The FAR has an established Code of Ethics and, additionally, requires its members to abide by a number of unwritten rules of conduct.

All ARs are precluded from carrying on any trade or business other than that of public accountancy. They may not be in salaried employment or hold any salaried office other than in a firm of public accountants. However, exemption from this embargo has traditionally been granted to ARs entering teaching posts. An AR must be strictly independent from any firm to which he is appointed as auditor and is precluded from having any interest therein. Although an appointment as auditor is always made to an individual AR, he may practise in sole trader, partnership or limited company form, provided that in the latter case, all the shareholders and board members are ARs. In addition to audit work, an AR is likely to be heavily involved in tax advice and consultancy work, and also to be employed on valuation work, investigations generally, government commissions, and may also act as an arbitrator, estate administrator or trustee.

The Approved Examiner of Accounts (GG) may be likened to a 'technician' accountant compared with the AR who is the 'technologist'. The GG must possess 'such knowledge and experience as will enable him to examine accounts and consider simple administrative questions connected with such examination'. In order to qualify as a GG, a candidate must be at least 25 years of age and of good character, possess a good knowledge of bookkeeping, the law relating to annual reports and taxation, and demonstrate his suitability for accountancy work. He may demonstrate his knowledge by means of a commercial school certificate or at least five years' practical experience in a responsible position as a clerk to an AR or in a large business firm. In the case of the GG also, approval is granted by a chamber of commerce.

Most GGs are members of the Swedish Accountants Association (Svenska Revisoramfundet) and are allowed to carry out audit work, although in the case of larger limited companies at least one of the company's auditors must be an AR. Unlike an AR, a GG may be in other, salaried, employment whilst he is also conducting audit work.

The appointment of auditor, other than in the case of larger limited companies, is not restricted to a qualified accountant. Any Swedish citizen can be appointed and, provided that permission is gained from the Royal Board of Trade, so can a foreign national. However, any appointment of auditors must be accompanied by the appointment of a similar number of deputies. Also, shareholders carrying over one-quarter (or one-third, in some cases) of the voting rights can appoint additional auditors together with deputies, even though the required number may already have been appointed.

There are currently about 1000 ARs and GGs carrying out audit work. They are concerned with approximately 100 companies quoted on the Stock Exchange, but most of their work is concerned with the majority of the 100000 or so unquoted limited companies which use their services either statutorily or voluntarily.

Statutory Requirements

The legislation regulating Swedish limited companies is the Bookkeeping Law 1929, the Companies Act 1944 and the Municipal Tax Law. The Companies Act prescribes a number of accounting practices and minimum standard financial statement classifications. It also states maximum valuation rules. Within these constraints both the Bookkeeping Law and the Companies Act state the rules to be applied are those 'in accordance with generally accepted accounting principles and sound business practice'. However, as taxable income is largely determined in accordance with actual financial book entries, sound business practice has traditionally been concerned with minimizing the profit figure in order to reduce the taxation liability. Accordingly, the lack of any minimum value rules, and the tax rules which have allowed the creation of asset reserves and income smoothing, have together resulted in the creation of secret reserves and an orientation towards the 'minimum position' in financial reporting. However, legislation now provides that material changes in accounting principles affecting the profit figure must be commented upon and the insured values of assets must be stated. The tax laws now allow different figures for tax and 'booked' depreciation and stipulate a maximum permitted stock reserve. Nevertheless, the financial statements are still creditor- and tax-orientated because of a backlog of old secret reserves and a continuing tendency towards income smoothing. The proposed company law reforms published in 1970 (see 'Current Trends') may go some way towards altering this situation in the case of quoted companies. The main requirements are outlined in the summary below.

Standards

Auditing

There are no codified auditing standards, but recommendations as to auditing practice are issued periodically by the FAR and the chambers of commerce. Minimum standards are contained in the Companies Act which specifically requires the auditor to examine:

1   The books and records.
2   Minutes of meetings of directors and shareholders.
3   Cash and other asset inventories.
4   The company's system of internal control.
5   The annual financial statements and report of the board.

In addition, the Act requires the auditor to examine and report upon the administration of the company's affairs, in order that the shareholders may annually discharge the board of management from responsibility. Maximum asset valuation rules are stipulated by the Companies Act, but tax legislation encourages lower valuations in practice (See 'Statutory Requirements' above). In a few cases the extent of income distortion brought about by the taxation rules is shown.

Reporting

There is no standard form of auditor's report. The Companies Act states that as well as signing (certifying) the balance sheet, the auditor must submit a separate report to the shareholders. This report is filed with the annual financial statements and must specifically refer to:

1   Any reservations of the auditor in connection with the company's financial statements, its bookkeeping, its assets and/or its administration.
2   The auditor's recommendations as to the adoption of the balance sheet, the discharge of management from further responsibility in connection with the current year, and his agreement to the proposed profit appropriations and distributions.
3   Any departure from the maximum valuation rules involving higher asset valuation.
4   His examination of certain legally required pension funds.

In the case of a parent company, his report must also refer to the fulfilment or otherwise of the legal requirements concerning information on shareholdings and subsidiaries' activities, and to the 'soundness' of any proposed dividend in connection with the group results and state of affairs.

The auditor's report, therefore, certifies compliance with the law. Although the requirement to certify the efficacy of the company's management could be interpreted as requiring an opinion, this certification is more likely to be a statement signifying that the administration has been carried out in accordance with the law and the company's statutes.

Accounting

Although the FAR has issued recommendations on accounting principles, the only mandatory standards are those contained in the Bookkeeping Law 1929 and the Companies Act 1944. Amendments in 1950 to the Companies Act had the effect of slightly reducing the extent of secrecy attaching to many reserves. They required:

1   The statement of property-tax assessments in relation to fixed property.
2   Disclosure of fire insurance valuations on fixed property, machinery and equipment.
3   A note of any changes in accounting principles which materially affected reported results for the year.

Although these amendments increased the information on asset values they still allowed the original reserves to remain hidden. The Bookkeeping Law and Companies Act state the maximum asset values which are acceptable, leaving any lower valuations to be reported where these 'are in accordance with generally accepted accounting principles and sound business practice'. These principles and practice have become orientated towards the 'minimum position' in financial statements through the preponderance of the concept of conservatism, creditor-orientation, and the linking of financial and taxable profits. Thus the 1955 tax legislation, by stipulating maxima for allowable stock reserves and depreciation rates, had the effect of fixing minimum values of assets for financial statements purposes. The tax laws also allow tax free reserves to be built up out of profits before tax. These reserves may subsequently be utilized at times when the government requires additional investment by firms, to combat local or national recessions. Thus, legal backing is given to a policy of 'income smoothing' rather than to 'true and fair' disclosure. Two other factors have influenced accounting standards. The first is the use, by many industries, of standard charts of accounts. The most well-known of these is that used by the Swedish Association of Metalworking Industries – the M chart. This has had a considerable influence on cost accounting and internal reporting standards generally, within Swedish firms. The second is a standard form of financial statements recently recommended by the FAR. This standard form is more orientated towards investor requirements. It considerably improves both the quantity and the quality of reported information given by those firms, mainly quoted companies, which have adopted it. Current practice is outlined in the summary.

Extra-statutory Requirements

There are few extra-statutory requirements relating to the accounting profession and the

Stock Exchange, and they are merely recommendations and not mandatory requirements.

Professional Bodies

The FAR has not yet issued any mandatory requirements although it has issued various recommendations on auditing, reporting and accounting matters. There are no codified auditing standards or accounting principles but the FAR has encouraged the provision of more and better financial information, and has recently recommended a standard form of financial statements for adoption by the larger companies.

Stock Exchange

The Swedish stock market is small, and there are only about 100 firms quoted on the Stockholm Stock Exchange. Most brokerage business is handled by the banks, 12 of the 18 brokerage houses being banks. However, in recent years there has been a considerable expansion in activity and a growth in public participation. It has been said that 'playing the market' has become something of a 'major sport and pastime'. Partly because of this growth, and also to encourage it, the Stock Exchange has issued some recommendations on the disclosure of information and financial statement presentation.

Financial reporting requirements The Council of the Stock Exchange may require information to be presented to it or published, in addition to that required by law. In general, however, its recommendations tend to be clarifications of existing legal requirements rather than additional controls.

Listing requirements and prospectuses Any application must be reviewed by the Council of the Stock Exchange and give details of the issue price, face value and method of payment of the shares to be issued. The company's annual report and the auditor's report for the last five years (two years in the case of bonds or debentures where the company's shares were not previously listed) must be submitted with the application. Normally, the application is handled by a bank, after being made in the first instance by the company management or a Stock Exchange member. The information to be provided to potential investors is largely at the discretion of the bank handling the transaction. Companies applying for a listing have to fulfil minimum capital requirements and these ensure, under the terms of the Companies Act, that at least one of the auditors is an AR.

Takeover and merger requirements There is no code of permissible practice covering takeovers and mergers. The only manner in which control would normally be exercised is under the overall review procedure of the Council of the Stock Exchange.

Summary of the Principal Areas of Current Accounting and Reporting Requirements in Sweden

Accountant's Report to be Included in a Prospectus for the Sale of Securities

There is no requirement for an independent accountant's report, nor for a profits forecast. The information to be provided to a prospective purchaser is largely determined by the commercial bank which will normally handle the sale of securities. The responsibility for the accuracy of the information rests upon the board of directors of the company and there are no legal requirements governing the contents of a prospectus. In order to grant a listing, the Council of the Stock Exchange would normally require: a minimum capital of S Kr 5 million (£500000); that shares be fully paid up; that share certificates are issued; and that the company must be liquid and solvent. In addition, the company's accounts, annual reports and auditor's reports for the last five years must also be submitted. In the case of a bond or debenture issue the submission of accounts and reports may be wholly or partially omitted.

Form and Content of Published Accounts

All companies must file a copy of the audited annual accounts consisting of a balance sheet, profit and loss account and directors' report, with the Royal Patent and Registration Office. Although there is no requirement for the accounts to be published, the filed copies are available for inspection by the general public, and many of the larger companies do send copies of their annual statements and reports to their shareholders.

There is no prescribed form of balance sheet but the Companies Act does contain requirements concerning classification and content. The following assets must be separately shown:

1 Unpaid share capital.
2 Fixed assets and intangibles, distinguishing goodwill, patents, organization costs, leaseholds, agricultural and forest property, other realty, machinery and equipment, securities other than shares, shares in subsidiaries and other shares.
3 Stocks.
4 Other current assets, distinguishing short-term securities other than shares, short-term shareholdings, amounts due from subsidiaries, loans to officers in excess of approximately £1000 or 2% of the capital, bills receivable, debtors and cash.
5 Any loss.

Liabilities must be separated as follows:

1 Capital.
2 Reserves, distinguishing between legal, other reserves, and deferred income.
3 Valuation reserves where not deducted from assets.
4 Long-term liabilities, distinguishing investment reserve, pension reserve, secured loans and others.
5 Short-term liabilities, distinguishing indebtedness to subsidiaries, bills payable and others.
6 Deferred taxes.
7 Any profit.

Where the information is not included on the face of the balance sheet, disclosure must be made of the amount of bills receivable discounted, any guarantees, and details of pledges, liens and securities given on real property, stocks and ships.

The Act places little emphasis on the profit and loss account other than requiring that as well as operating income (showing differentiation between product lines, if not injurious to the company), there should be separately shown:

1   Share dividends received (separating subsidiaries' dividends from others).
2   Interest received (similarly distinguished).
3   Extraordinary income.
4   Interest incurred.
5   Direct taxes.
6   Depreciation (distinguished according to class of asset).
7   General and administrative expenses (including fees to management and auditors).
8   Extraordinary expenses (including provisions and reserves).

There is no legal requirement for consolidated accounts or statements to be presented to shareholders or to be filed with the annual accounts. However, there are requirements for:

1   The managing director to present to the board and to the auditors a consolidated balance sheet or group statement showing the result of the group's operations.
2   The group profit/loss for the year and the group's accumulated profits and free reserves to be stated in the report of management and thereby be available for inspection.
3   The auditors, when referring in their report to the soundness of the proposed distributions, to consider expressly the results of the group as a whole.

In addition, shareholders must be given the following information:

1   Inter-company shareholdings and indebtedness.
2   Inter-company contingent liabilities and securities granted.
3   The extent and nature of a parent company's shareholding in subsidiaries.
4   The latest balance sheet of each subsidiary.

There is no standard form of audit report but the Companies Act does require that, as well as signing the balance sheet and profit and loss account, the auditor must present a separate report. The matters to be included in this report are specified, and include the following:

1   The results of the audit and particularly any reservations of the auditor concerning the accounts, the bookkeeping, the safeguarding of the assets and/or the administration of the company's affairs.
2   The reasons for any such reservations.
3   The auditor's recommendations as to the adoption of the balance sheet and the discharge of the board and managing director from further responsibility concerning the current year's financial statements.

4   The auditor's agreement with the proposed profit appropriations and distributions.
5   Any write-up of assets above cost, and the correctness of any legally required pension funds.
6   Compliance with the requirements of the Act concerning information on subsidiaries and group results.

A directors' report – a 'report on the administration' – must be submitted to the auditors for their review and report, presented to the shareholders, and filed with the annual financial statements. The report must include, where the information is not stated elsewhere, details of:

1   Assessed values of real property for tax purposes, and insured values of real property, machinery and plant for fire insurance purposes.
2   Details of the average numbers and total salaries of manual workers, management and others.
3   Details of any asset write-up above cost.
4   Proposed profit appropriations.
5   Details of group profits and other information required about subsidiaries.
6   Material effects of changes and accounting policies.
7   Provided it does not prejudice the company, details of net sales, changes in the company's activities or policies which are of note, and any important post-date events.

Current Practice

Fixed assets Undervaluation of fixed assets is permitted by current Swedish law in that it only stipulates maximum value. This value is stated as being cost. Special depreciation allowances or accelerated depreciation rates may be used to reduce an asset to 'true value' where this is below net book value. Fixed assets may be written up to their 'enduring value' (not to exceed the property-tax assessed value in the case of real property), where this materially exceeds net book value, provided that:

1   The write-up can be utilized in a corresponding writing down of other assets, or
2   It is accompanied by a bonus issue of shares to increase capital by a similar amount.

The amount of any such write-up and its treatment must be disclosed in the report of management. The value assessed for property-tax purposes, and the value of the asset for fire insurance purposes must be disclosed. Depreciation charged in the financial accounts need not correspond with the taxation rules although, in practice, it frequently does. Tax law allows up to 30% pa to be written off book values of most fixed property (machinery may be written off over five years) and, in some cases, this allowance can run from the date on which a contract to purchase was signed rather than the date on which the asset first came into use. Best practice discloses the effect of charging accelerated depreciation, where this is not based upon the asset's useful life, although there is no requirement in law to do so. There is no standard form of treatment of fixed assets in the balance sheet: the Companies Act recommends that accumulated depreciation should be shown as a separate depreciation reserve, the FAR recommends that it be shown as a deduction from the gross value of the asset, whilst, in practice, many firms merely show the values net of accumulated depreciation. Finally, fixed assets with an expected lifetime not exceeding three years need not be capitalized.

Goodwill and intangibles Goodwill, which can only be shown as the result of a transaction cost, may be written off over a period not exceeding ten years. Tax law stipulates a maximum period of five years. Other intangibles may be written off over their useful lives.

Investments Investments must be shown at a figure not exceeding the lower of cost or market value, although they may, in fact, appear at a much lower value where management deems that 'sound business practice' requires it. Separate information concerning investments in subsidiaries must be given (see 'Form and Content of Published Accounts'), but the valuation rules are the same.

Current assets and stocks Values must not exceed the lower of cost or market price. Stock values may be further reduced by:

1   Up to 60% of the lower price (the reduction being calculated either on the current inventory or on the average stockholding during the two previous years), or
2   An amount which would reduce the value of raw materials or staple commodities to a minimum figure of 70% of the lowest market price of those materials or commodities at any time during the previous nine years.

For these deductions to apply for tax allowance they must be used in the preparation of the financial profit figures. Stocks normally include overheads and would be calculated according to the FIFO method. Methods of showing any stock reserve vary in practice, best practice disclosing the amount. Legislation does require the effect of any material change in policy concerning the stock reserve to be disclosed. Debtors may be reduced by, or have a reserve for, any specific amounts deemed to be worthless. A general percentage reserve is not permitted. Any reduction of the debtors figure is not legally required to be shown. Loans to directors over £1000 and indebtedness to subsidiaries are shown separately.

Deferred charges Capitalization of formation expenses is not allowed. Other deferred charges are normally written off over the period to which the charges relate. Expenses incurred in establishing a new product, such as advertising or research and development, would normally be written off over a period not exceeding five years.

Liabilities Long-term liabilities have to be distinguished from short-term liabilities, the dividing line normally being whether or not the liabilities are due to be met within one year. Details of property mortgaged as security for liabilities must be disclosed but there is no requirement for details of terms and duration of loans to be given.

Reserves and provisions A legal reserve is required under Swedish Company Law. This reserve consists of a basic annual appropriation of 10% of net income until the reserve is equivalent to 20% of the issued share capital. In addition, where the company's liabilities exceed the total of issued capital and legal reserves, a special legal reserve is required. This special legal reserve must, like the normal legal reserve, be built up by annual appropriations of 10% of net income even though the normal reserve may already amount to 20% of issued share capital. The legal reserve may only be utilized to reduce a deficit and only then when other 'free' reserves have been exhausted. Where the special legal reserve exceeds requirements, any excess may be transferred to free reserves, in total, where the excess has been in existence continuously throughout the last five years, or at the rate of 20% each year in other cases. Dividends must be restricted to 5% of the net assets where liabilities exceed the total of share capital and legal reserves, unless an equivalent amount to the excess over 5% is added to the legal reserves. Any share premium must be added to the normal legal reserve. The proposed company law reforms (see 'Current Trends') dispense with the legal reserves. Any company which has lost two-thirds of its share capital must:

1   Prepare a liquidation balance sheet using mainly net realizable values.
2   Call a meeting of shareholders to consider the position if this loss is confirmed by the liquidation balance sheet.
3   Either make good the loss within four months of the meeting or apply to liquidate the company.

Many firms build up an Investment Fund Reserve by means of appropriations of up to 40% of pretax profits in order to 'stabilize' future earnings figures. In order to qualify for tax exemption, any such build up must be accompanied by cash investment of 46% of each transfer in a blocked interest-free account with the Swedish Central Bank.

These reserves are released at times when the government, through the Royal Labour Market Board, wishes to stimulate economic investment on the part of firms. Any assets purchased under such conditions qualify for tax allowances on the cost price less any of the reserve used towards its purchase. Assets purchased under these conditions are often brought into account at this net figure rather than cost.

Other 'free' or distributable reserves are often maintained, and valuation reserves, including accumulated depreciation, are frequently shown both within and outside shareholders' equity. Secret reserves are commonplace in spite of attempts by the Companies Act amendment to make them less secret. Only material increases or decreases in these reserves need to be commented upon by the directors, and any attempt to assess the absolute amount of any reserve requires a reliance on the figures given for tax assessment and fire insurance purposes. In the case of assets other than fixed property, even this insight is not available. However, some of the larger companies are beginning to show movements on reserves.

Share capital Shares must be registered, have a minimum par value, and be fully paid up within two years of registration. A company must have a minimum share capital of at least S Kr 5000 (£500) and is prohibited from purchasing its own shares. Any premium on shares must be put to the legal reserve, and any unpaid share capital is shown as an asset. Shareholders' equity is not necessarily shown as one figure on the balance sheet. Bonus issues are normally shown at par. Dividends (proposed) may not be shown in the accounts but must be stated as a recommendation in the report of management.

Accounting for aquisitions and mergers There is little standard practice and pooling of interests method is not recognized in Sweden.

Income statement Turnover must be disclosed in the report of management if not stated in the profit and loss account. Operating income must be shown, allocated between the firm's activities, if appropriate. A company may be exempted from disclosing a sales figure or segregated income figures where it would be prejudicial to the company's interests. Cost of sales would not, normally, be shown. Total remuneration of employees, separating manual workers, management and other employees, must be stated in the management report, if not included in the income statement. Similarly, average numbers of employees must be stated. Depreciation must be shown, allocated according to asset groupings. General administrative expenses must be shown although, in the absence of any legal guidelines, there is considerable difference in practice as to the items to be included. Interest and dividends received and paid must be separately shown, further distinction being made between that relating to subsidiaries and other interest and dividends. Taxation accounting is normal practice although some differences may arise in connection with depreciation charges. Although best practice often discloses the extent of tax distortion of reported profit, it is unlikely that any attempt would be made to account for deferred taxation liabilities. Profits and losses on the sale of fixed assets, and extraordinary items must be separately shown. Appropriations are often not shown as a separate section, transfers to reserves being made through the profit and loss account. The FAR has recommended the use of a separate 'Appropriations' section. Proposed dividends are not normally shown in the income statement.

Other points The financial accounts may only serve to show the 'minimum position', the overriding concept being conservatism and the most important influence being tax legislation. Best practice does give some insight into the extent of secret reserves, and changes therein, and of the main tax distortions. Notes to the accounts are sparingly used since considerable detail is required in the report of management. The effect of material changes in accounting policies and any post-date events would be disclosed. Contingent liabilities must be stated, but there is no requirement for capital commitments to be shown. Comparative figures are often shown, although there is no legal requirement to do so.

Current Trends

Two factors seem to be paramount in the changing Swedish accounting 'climate'. The first of these is the increased interest of the general public in, and the rapidly expanded activity of, the stock market. The second is the attempt to harmonize Scandinavian company laws in anticipation of an eventual harmonization of European company law generally. These moves may be seen in statutory and professional trends as well as in other areas.

Statutory Trends

The main statutory trend is that of the proposed company law reform. Proposals were first published in Sweden in late 1970 and are gradually being implemented by means of periodic amendments to the 1944 Companies Act. Some of the most significant proposals from the viewpoint of Swedish accounting practice are:

1   The abolition of the compulsory legal reserve.
2   The inclusion of notes to the financial statements as an integral part of the annual accounts to be audited and filed.
3   The requirement for consolidated balance sheets to be prepared, although not necessarily for public dissemination in that form.
4   The inclusion of a model (although not prescribed) set of financial statements involving a standard classification for shareholders' equity, treatment of reserves and depreciation provisions, treatment of losses, information on associated and subsidiary companies, and a more informative form of profit and loss statement.

The proposals do not prohibit the existence or creation of secret reserves, but do require publication of certain explanatory information relevant to asset valuations. In general, the proposed reforms will give statutory backing to what is currently best accounting practice in Sweden.

To coincide with the proposed company law reforms, two other laws are currently being revised. Firstly, the 1929 Bookkeeping Law is being updated to make it more relevant to present day accounting methods and the increased information requirements of the new companies' legislation. Secondly, a law regulating the provision of information to be provided by companies quoted on the Stockholm Stock Exchange is in draft. This law will require:

1   The publication of a consolidated balance sheet and profit and loss account.
2   The provision of interim reports.
3   Disclosures as to the amount and extent of asset under-valuations.

These rules will apply also to all limited companies employing more than 500 persons, whether the firm's shares are quoted or not.

Professional Trends

The role of the FAR in recommending and promoting best practice has already been referred to in the section on accounting standards. In response to the increased public interest in the stock market, the profession is actively encouraging the shift in orientation of financial reporting away from creditors and more towards investors' needs. The main evidence for this is seen in the recommended form of financial statements and, particularly, in the increased emphasis placed on information to be given in the earnings statement.

Other Trends

The growth in interest and participation in stock market activities is accompanied by an increasing similarity between the objectives of private and public enterprises. Both are beginning to show a willingness to cooperate with government and other state and local authorities in order to benefit the community as a whole. This is particularly so in the case of the larger private companies whose increasing capital requirements, both in terms of domestic and foreign finance, are likely to involve them in better disclosure of information in order to promote their 'good corporate image'.

Until very recently, the accounting system in Sweden was the archetype of Mueller's macroeconomic pattern as described in Chapter 1. Currently, despite the pressures for a more pronounced orientation towards the provision of information geared to investors' needs, many of the practices developed in accordance with this pattern still remain. The most noticeable of these are the continuing practices of 'income smoothing', under-valuation of assets, and the congruence between financial and taxation reporting.

13

Switzerland

Type of Business Unit

Companies with Limited Liability

In general, business units are governed by Swiss federal laws, and by particular cantonal requirements according to the location of the enterprise. The federal Code of Obligations of 1911 – as amended in 1936 – is the main statute governing limited liability companies. Limited liability companies are comprised of:

1   Public companies (Aktiengesellschaft or Société Anonyme – AG or SA). These corporations must have a minimum of three founder members, and, after incorporation, there must be at least three shareholders. There is a minimum share capital requirement of S Fr 50000 (£7000), of which at least S Fr 20000 (£2800) – or 20% of the share capital if greater – must be paid up, and there is a minimum share value of S Fr 100 (£14). Shares may be registered or, if fully paid up, bearer. All shares must be subscribed, there being no facility for authorized but unissued share capital, and a company may restrict ownership or transferability of shares. Directors must hold qualifying shares, and either a majority of them or the sole director must fulfil residence and nationality requirements. Directors are initially appointed for a maximum period of three years following incorporation, thereafter for six-year terms. All corporations must appoint a statutory auditor. Additionally, a company which has share capital in excess of S Fr 5 million (£700000), or has debentures outstanding, or has obtained funds from the public, must appoint a professional independent accountant (who may also be the statutory auditor). Quoted companies must file the annual

report and audited accounts with the Stock Exchange, and banks and insurance companies must publish audited annual accounts in the official gazette. Apart from the above, there are no filing or publishing requirements concerning the audited annual financial accounts.

2   Private companies (Gesellschaft mit beschranker Haftung or Société à résponsabilité limitée – GMBH or SARL). These companies must have at least two members on formation but this may later fall to one. Capital must be at least S Fr 20000 (£2800) but may not exceed S Fr 2 million (£280000). Individual members' shares must be at least S Fr 1000 (£143) and in multiples of S Fr 1000. Each member must pay in at least one-half of the nominal value of his share, and may be liable up to the amount of the registered capital. Each member is also liable to make good any unsubscribed capital of any other member. No share certificates are issued and at least three-quarters of the members – in number and in capital value – must agree to any transfer of interest. At least one manager who is a Swiss resident (but not necessarily a Swiss national) must be appointed by the members. There are no statutory requirements covering the preparation, filing or publishing of annual accounts, nor for the appointment of statutory auditor. This form of organization is not popular in Switzerland because members cannot shelter under a cloak of anonymity as in the case of the AG and also because of the maximum capital limitation.

Cooperatives

Cooperatives (Genossenschaft or Société cooperative) are a common form of business organization, mainly used for building, agricultural and retail distribution purposes. They do not have a fixed capital. A member's individual liability is restricted to the amount of his contributed capital, and that of the cooperative is limited to its own assets. Cooperatives must appoint a statutory auditor.

Partnerships

Partnerships may be:

1   General (Kollectivgesellschaft or Société en nom collectif) which is the normal commercial form involving joint and several liability of the partners.
2   Limited (Kommanditgesellschaft or Société en commandite) which requires at least one unlimited partner who must be an individual. Any form of entity or individual may become a limited partner, but as is usual in this form of organization they may not participate in the firm's management.
3   Limited by shares (Kommanditaktiengesellschaft or Société en commandite par actions). This form is very similar to that of the limited partnership but limited partners are only liable to the extent of the nominal value of their share subscriptions. The unlimited partners form the board of directors, the limited partners may appoint a supervisory board. This form of organization is, in other respects, governed by the laws relating to limited companies but it is rarely used in practice.
4   Civil (Einfache gesellschaft or Société Simple). This is similar to a joint venture and is not regarded legally as a commercial organization. It may include a limited company as one of its general partners.

Sole Traders with Unlimited Liability

Branches of Foreign Enterprises

A branch of a foreign enterprise must register with the Registrar of Commerce in the canton in which it is situated. A Swiss resident, who need not be of Swiss nationality, must be appointed as the branch manager, and full details of the head office organization must also be registered and extracts published in the official gazette. A branch must keep a full and separate set of accounting records. This form of organization is not very popular because of the amount of documentation required (often increased in particular cantons), the need for registration of head office particulars, and the requirement that the head office must undertake responsibility to discharge all the branch liabilities.

Business Records

The Code of Obligations requires that proper books of account be kept. These are not prescribed but must be such 'as a prudent businessman would keep'. They must be adequate for the type and size of operations, and in particular they must:

1 Reveal the financial position of the firm through inclusion of all debits and credits connected with the business.
2 Show the results of operations on an annual basis.
3 Allow the preparation of annual accounts which are complete, thorough and clear.

In addition, various laws require that records should be maintained:

1 For social security purposes.
2 On taxes withheld.
3 For taxation purposes.

The Accounting Profession

The accounting profession in Switzerland is largely based on a two-tier system. The lower tier is made up of the Union of Federally Certified Book-keepers (Vereinigung Eidgenossischer Diplomierter Buchhalter) who are normally employed in commerce or industry as book-keepers/accountants rather than as independent auditors.

The higher tier is made up of those accountants, professionally qualified by examination or experience or both, who are organized under the control of the Swiss Chamber of Fiduciaries and Auditors (Schweizerische Treuhand und Revisionskammer or Chambre Suisse des Sociétés Fiduciaires et des Experts-Comptables). It is this body which largely makes up the accounting profession in Switzerland as regards auditing, reporting and accounting.

The Swiss Auditing Chamber (formed in 1925) is a national association comprised of three bodies:

1   The Society of Swiss Certified Accountants (Verband Schweizerischer Bucherexperten or Associations Suisse des Experts-Comptables – VSB).
2   The Union of Fiduciary and Auditing Firms (Union des Sociétés Fiduciaires).
3   The Group of Audit Associations for Banks and Savings Banks.

Of these three bodies, the VSB is the only one to require its members to undergo a formal programme of examination and experience.

The Society was formed in 1913 and has a current membership of approximately 700. To qualify as a VSB a person must pass preliminary and final examinations involving a knowledge of auditing, economics, law and taxation. He must also, as part of the final examination, solve a professionally orientated problem which demonstrates a knowledge of auditing, business mathematics, statistics and business organization. The examination is held every two years, under the control of the Ministry of Economics, but administered by the Swiss Auditing Chamber. In addition to passing the examinations, the would-be VSB must have at least six years' relevant experience: the first three in accounting and including at least two years' auditing experience, prior to his sitting the preliminary examination and a further three years before he can sit for his final examination. The title of Certified Accountant (Diplomierter Bucherexperte or Expert-Comptable) is protected and reserved for those persons passing the above examinations. However, the practice of accounting and auditing is not so reserved. A VSB must abide by the ethical rules of the society which are largely concerned with independence and with professional conduct. A VSB may practise in any type of civil or commercial organization, including a public limited company. He is likely to be engaged on statutory and independent audits, accountancy and management consultancy, taxation services and consultancy, investigatory and industrial analysis work, executorship and trustee work. He may also take up an appointment as a director (provided he is not also a statutory auditor to the same firm) and/or some other formal appointment concerned with company management.

The other two bodies making up the Swiss Auditing Chamber are associations of firms. Swiss fiduciary and auditing firms are nearly all public limited companies, and the services they offer include all those outlined above in respect of the VSB. To become a member of the Union, a fiduciary and auditing firm must be a legal entity separate from its members and have a capital of at least S Fr 100000 (£14000). A member of the Audit Associations for Banks and Savings Banks is likely to specialize in this type of work and must be approved by the Federal Banking Commission. This approval is required, in the case of bank audits, under the Federal Banking Law 1934 and, in the case of investment company audits, under the Federal Law on Investment Companies 1966. Apart from the specialist audit associations, about twenty fiduciary and auditing firms are also members of the Group.

Although independent professional accountants are specifically required to conduct an audit of the public limited company, this function is not specifically reserved to members of the bodies making up the Swiss Auditing Chamber. The independent professional auditor may also be appointed as the same firm's statutory auditor, but where these positions are held by separate persons or firms, the professional auditor must report to the statutory auditor. Unlike the statutory auditor, the professional is neither appointed by, nor is accountable to, the shareholders. The statutory auditor, on the other hand, does not need to be qualified, and the only legal requirements to be met are that:

1   He must notify his acceptance of the office to the Registry of Commerce.
2   He may not be an employee or a director of the company for which he is the auditor.

Statutory Requirements

The main statutory requirements governing limited liability companies, and in particular auditing, reporting and accounting matters, are contained in the Code of Obligations of 1911 as amended in 1936. The code requires the appointment of statutory auditors and stipulates their duties. It also specifies the circumstances in which an independent professional accountant is to be appointed. Standards to be used for reporting and accounting purposes are also contained in the code. The auditor must certify the correctness of the company's financial condition as stated in the books, and the annual accounts must be in accordance with generally accepted commercial principles and be complete, thorough and clear. Valuation principles are prescribed by the code. The requirements contained in the code tend to be general and permissive in nature. As a result, a number of other statutes have also stated requirements which either supplement or override its requirements. The most influential and frequently encountered of these are the tax laws which require items to be charged in the financial accounts before they can be allowed for tax purposes. Thus, most annual accounts are tax-orientated. Other statutes which govern companies formed for specific purposes include the Federal Banking Law 1934 and the Federal Law on Investment Companies 1966. Current requirements related to the preparation of accounts and disclosure of information are set out in the summary below.

Standards

Auditing

To date, no auditing standards have been issued, even as recommendations. Accordingly, audit standards vary considerably in practice. Minimum standards exist in the requirements of the Code of Obligations which defines the legal duties of the statutory auditor. These duties consist of:

1   Certifying that the profit and loss account and balance sheet agree with the books and records maintained by the company.
2   Certifying that those books and records have been properly kept.
3   Certifying that the financial statements and books and records have been prepared in accordance with the Code of Obligations and any special provisions contained in the company's statutes or articles.

The code also specifies those circumstances in which an independent professional accountant, who may or may not also act as the statutory auditor, must be appointed. Thus an independent professional accountant must be appointed by any corporation which:

1   Invites the public to subscribe capital.
2   Has a share capital of S Fr 5 million (£700 000) or more.
3   Has outstanding debentures.

A similar appointment must be made where a company is reducing its share capital without making the reduction good by a new issue of fully paid-up capital. In this case, the
professional auditor is required to be a member of the Union of Fiduciary and Auditing
Firms or of the Group of Auditing Associations. A member of the latter group must be
appointed for the purpose of conducting a bank audit.

   Except in the case of a bank appointment, a statutory auditor is allowed to maintain a
financial interest, such as a shareholding, in the company he audits. However, he may not
be a director or an employee of the audited company.

Reporting

Such reporting standards as exist are contained entirely within the Code of Obligations.
The statutory auditor must examine the financial statements and certify that they agree
with the books, that they accord with legal requirements and the company's own articles,
and that proper books have been kept. His report is made to the shareholders and must
recommend that the balance sheet be accepted, with or without qualification, or be re-
jected. In addition, he must advise the shareholders on the propriety or otherwise of the
directors' proposals for the distribution of profit. The report is usually in short form and
may be given separately from the statements reported upon. There is no standard form of
report. Where the auditor is a certified accountant, he may well present a long-form
report to the directors, in addition to the short report submitted to shareholders. Such a
report would include a discussion of his audit findings and of the important items in the
financial statements. It may also outline the audit procedures used. In the case of an independent professional accountant's report, where statutorily required, it would always be
in long form, contain the items outlined above, and be made to the directors and the
statutory auditor. In no case is the auditor, statutory or otherwise, legally required to
examine or comment upon the directors' report, other than in connection with their proposals concerning the profit distribution.

Accounting

In general, accounting standards in use are those which are in accordance with 'recognized commercial principles'. Although the Swiss Auditing Chamber has published some
reports making recommendations on accounting matters, they are not regarded as
mandatory. The standards obtaining are those contained in the legislation. The Code of
Obligations requires that annual accounts are prepared in Swiss currency and that they
should be complete, thorough and clear, although no prescribed format is given. The
code states that assets may not be valued at more than their worth to the business and
specific valuation principles are given. However, these principles are maximum values
only, and the code specifically allows undisclosed reserves and the under-valuation of
assets. The purpose of this is to ensure the continued prosperity of a company and permit
a uniform distribution of dividends. The effect of this requirement is to promote 'income-

smoothing' and creditor-orientated principles to the annual accounts so that they record only the 'minimum position'.

In addition to the requirements of the code, outlined above, tax legislation requires commonality between charges against both taxable and financial profits. There is thus an added incentive to undervalue assets, in order to claim accelerated depreciation and stock adjustments for tax purposes. This adds a tax orientation to the figures reported in the annual accounts. In the case of banking and investment companies, separate legislation prescribes a particular balance sheet format, although the general principles outlined above also apply. Current accounting requirements and practice are contained in the summary below.

Extra-statutory Requirements

The Swiss stock market is small and somewhat insignificant and only about 300 Swiss registered companies have shares traded on the Swiss stock exchanges. There is little private and equity investment for two main reasons. Firstly, firms tend to finance their policies internally. Secondly, Swiss company shares are relatively expensive to buy (few shares listed on the Zurich Stock Exchange are quoted at less than S Fr 1000 – £143 each). In addition, the banks are entitled to vote on the shares deposited with them, and most banks have representatives on company boards. There has, therefore, been little need for publicly available information for investors, since most investors are 'insiders'. Thus the growth of bodies designed to protect potential investors by means of self-imposed regulations is in a very early stage of development.

Professional Bodies

The Swiss Auditing Chamber is actively interested in promoting generally accepted accounting principles and has issued some recommendations which are neither commonly used nor intended to be mandatory. To date, it has issued no recommendations on auditing standards.

Stock Exchange

The Swiss Federal Association of Stock Exchanges is the body which administers the legal requirements of the Code of Obligations governing the listing of securities. However, the Association has also requested quoted firms to disclose more information in their financial statements. Although it is intended that the requirement will eventually be mandatory, firms currently supply the information on a voluntary basis only.

Financial reporting requirements In addition to the information statutorily required in annual accounts the association has recommended quoted companies to provide consolidated statements or group accounts. It has also requested firms to disclose details of their turnover, capital expenditures, numbers of employees in classified groupings, aggregate wages and salaries, fringe benefits, taxes, valuation and depreciation principles, and comparative figures.

Listing requirements and prospectuses Applications for listing are submitted through banks who are authorized stock exchange agents. The association administers the legal requirements although in 1969 it issued its own regulations governing 'third market' trading of unlisted securities.

Takeover and Merger Requirements

There are no extra-statutory requirements concerning takeovers and mergers.

Summary of the Principal Areas of Current Accounting and Reporting Requirements in Switzerland

Accountant's Report to be Included in a Prospectus for the Sale of Securities

There is no requirement for an independent accountant's report, nor for a profits forecast to be included. The law requires a prospectus to be published and a copy to be sent to the Stock Exchange, in which the following information must be included:

1   Company particulars and details of capital, reserves, unpaid capital, voting rights, secured debts outstanding and dividends paid during the last five years.
2   Names of directors and statutory auditors, and details of the company's most important subsidiaries, including their capitals and secured debts.
3   Copies of the last balance sheet and profit and loss account, together with a summary of operations since the date of the last annual accounts.
4   Terms and purpose of the issue.

Copies of the last published annual report, articles of association and existing share certificate(s) must be lodged with the Stock Exchange. A company statement and report on its financial position and operations must be deposited with the bank handling the application for use by the bank's shareholders. Copies of subsequent annual reports are required to be sent to the Stock Exchange and it must be notified of any changes in the company's articles. The total nominal value of a company's securities must be at least S Fr 500000 (£70000) in the case of a domestic issue and S Fr 1 million for a foreign issue.

Form and Content of Published Accounts

Quoted companies must file a copy of the annual audited accounts consisting of a balance sheet, profit and loss account, and the statutory auditor's report. A copy of the directors' annual report must also be filed in the case of a quoted company. There are no requirements for accounts to be published other than in the case of banking, investment and insurance companies. In these cases an abridged form of annual accounts must be published in the official gazette. There is no prescribed form of balance sheet nor any requirements as to classification and content. The only requirement is that the balance sheet should be 'complete, clear, neatly arranged and in accordance with recognized commercial principles'. Similarly, the only requirement concerning the profit and loss account is that it should be presented as part of the annual accounts and be drawn up in line with the same general principles applying to the balance sheet. Consolidated financial statements are not required, although some firms do present consolidated information voluntarily. Investments in subsidiaries are shown at cost or less.

The statutory auditors' report, which may be separate from the financial statements, is normally very brief and certifies that:

1 Proper books and records have been kept.
2 The financial statements agree with those books and records.
3 The financial statements, books and records comply with the law and the company's articles.

His report must recommend, qualify or advise the rejection of the financial statements by the shareholders, and must refer to the propriety or otherwise of the directors' proposals for profit distribution. An independent professional accountant's report would be in long form and submitted to the directors and statutory auditor (if a separate person from the professional accountant). It is not available to the shareholders unless the directors specifically allow it to be made available to them.

A directors' report – a business report – must be made, in writing, to the shareholders. This report must comment on the financial position of the company, its activities and its results over the year. The report must also contain the directors' proposals concerning profit distributions and appropriations.

Current Practice

Fixed assets Undervaluation of fixed assets is specifically permitted by Swiss law in the interests of the continued prosperity of the company and/or the maintenance of uniform dividend distributions. The legal valuation rules are maximum rules only. Fixed assets generally may not be valued in excess of cost less 'appropriate' depreciation. The depreciation rates are likely to be accelerated in accordance with tax rules rather than based on the asset's useful life because of the stipulation that tax allowances cannot exceed 'booked' depreciation. Depreciation on real property may be charged before the property is in use. The bases of asset valuation are not normally disclosed, although, where assets are insured against fire risks, the insured amount must be stated on the balance sheet. Amounts set aside as depreciation are often accumulated as reserves shown on the liabilities side of the balance sheet, the corresponding assets being shown at their gross amounts.

Goodwill and intangibles These must not be shown in excess of cost and must be 'appropriately' amortized. What is 'appropriate' is normally governed by the tax laws.

Investments Investments in quoted securities must not be valued at more than their average quoted value during the month preceding the date of the balance sheet. Where the quotation is only available outside Switzerland, a deduction must be made for any anticipated costs of transfer. Unquoted securities must not exceed cost price plus any accrued income and/or less any reserve for loss in value.

Current assets and stocks Current assets must generally not be valued in excess of the lower of cost or net realisable value. Stocks must be valued in accordance with the above rule but there is no restriction in the valuation rules regarding a minimum value. In practice, stocks are frequently undervalued. Some limitations on deductions are provided by the tax laws. These state that where sufficiently detailed stock records are maintained to identify individual prices and quantities, minimum acceptable values for tax purposes are two-thirds of the lower of cost or market prices. Stocks are usually costed at average, direct cost. Debtors, if irrecoverable, are usually deducted, although there is no requirement in the valuation rules covering general provisions. Any provision against bad debts might, however, be shown with the liabilities.

Deferred charges The general rule is that deferred charges should be written off to profit and loss account in the year in which they are incurred. The tax laws do allow certain formation expenses, where authorized by the company's articles and shareholders, to be carried forward and amortized over a period not exceeding five years.

Liabilities It is usual to separate current liabilities from those which are medium- and long-term. Specifically secured or guaranteed liabilities are not required to be shown separately from general liabilities. Details of securities given are normally shown but the period and terms of liabilities are seldom disclosed. The total of redemption prices of debentures must be separately shown on the liabilities side of the balance sheet.

Reserves and provisions A legal reserve is required of at least 20% of paid-up share capital and until this amount is accumulated, 5% of the profit after tax must be appropriated annually. Share premiums, unless they are used to depreciate assets or for staff welfare purposes, must be placed to the legal reserve. Except in the case of holding companies, an amount equivalent to 10% of the excess of any distribution over 5% of the paid-up capital must be transferred to the legal reserve. A legal reserve, to the extent that it does not exceed 50% of the issued share capital, can only be used to cover losses. This restriction is waived in the case of holding companies. When the accumulated deficit of a company is greater than 50% of the paid-up capital, a meeting of shareholders must be called in order to note the position and to recommend appropriate action. Secret reserves are commonplace and are specifically permitted in order to ensure the continued prosperity of the business and/or to permit the distribution of uniform dividends. They are most likely to originate from the undervaluation of fixed assets, stocks and investments. The statutory auditor must be informed of variations in these reserves, but is not normally allowed to pass on any information or comment in his report to shareholders. Provision must be made in the accounts for all anticipated losses.

Share capital All shares must have a minimum nominal value of S Fr 100 (£14), and, if fully paid up, may be in bearer form. There must be a minimum share capital of S Fr 50 000 (£7000) and at least 20% of the share capital must be paid up. Any unpaid share capital is shown as an asset. Share capital must be fully subscribed; authorized but unissued capital is not permitted. A company is not normally allowed to purchase its own shares and, where this is allowed, the shares must either be cancelled or disposed of as soon as possible. Shareholders' equity is not required to be shown. Dividends proposed are not shown in the accounts, the proposals being included in the directors' report for shareholders' adoption. Bonus issues of shares are not permitted.

Accounting for acquisitions and mergers The pooling of interests method of accounting for acquisitions and mergers is not used, and merged company assets are recorded in accordance with tax legislation.

Income statement Some turnover and operating statistics may be shown but these are not required by law, and are therefore seldom disclosed in a useful form. Depreciation must be shown although, since tax allowances cannot exceed 'book' depreciation, it is more likely to be based on tax considerations than on the useful life of the assets. Although there may be some differences between 'booked' and 'tax-allowable' expenses, deferred taxation is not accrued. In some cases, tax arising on reported earnings but not actually assessed, is not included as an accrual in the accounts. Directors' bonuses are not allowable for tax purposes and are therefore usually shown as appropriations of net profit.

Other points Notes need not form an integral part of the accounts and any that are given are likely to appear on the face of the balance sheet. The only item that has to be shown is the amount of any material contingent liabilities. There is no requirement to show the bases used for individual items in the accounts and, although changes in bases are allowed provided that they do not result in an overstatement of the financial position, the effect of these changes would not be disclosed. There are no requirements to disclose capital commitments or material after-date events.

Current Trends

Statutory Trends

A government committee is working on company law reform, but this is in a relatively early stage and no recommendations have yet been published. In addition, a working party has been constituted to study auditors' competence and independence.

Professional Trends

The Swiss Auditing Chamber is to issue guidelines on auditing standards. Although these guidelines will not be mandatory, they should have the effect of reducing the variety of auditing standards currently practised and also of increasing both the quantity and the quality of information to be included in annual financial statements.

Other Trends

The Swiss Federal Association of Stock Exchanges has requested all quoted firms to disclose more information in their financial statements (See 'Extra-statutory Requirements'). Although this increased information is only provided currently on a voluntary basis, the stated intention of the association is ultimately to make the requirements mandatory.

The accounting system in Switzerland is still in a very early stage of development. No clearly identifiable pattern seems to have emerged although elements both of the micro-economic and pragmatic patterns identified by Mueller and described in Chapter 1 can be seen. Trends seem to suggest that further development will follow a distinct macro-orientation.

Index